LIFE ON TOUR
WITH
BOWIE

LIFE ON TOUR
WITH
BOWIE

A GENIUS REMEMBERED

SEAN MAYES

MUSIC
PRESS

Published by Music Press Books
an imprint of John Blake Publishing Ltd,
3 Bramber Court, 2 Bramber Road,
London W14 9PB, England

www.johnblakebooks.com

www.facebook.com/johnblakebooks 🄵
twitter.com/jblakebooks 🅃

This edition published in 2016

ISBN: 978 1 78418 975 4

British Library Cataloguing-in-Publication Data:

A catalogue record for this book is available from the British Library.

Design by www.envydesign.co.uk

Printed in Great Britain by CPI Group (UK) Ltd

1 3 5 7 9 10 8 6 4 2

Papers used by John Blake Publishing are natural, recyclable products made from
wood grown in sustainable forests. The manufacturing processes conform to the
environmental regulations of the country of origin.

Every attempt has been made to contact the relevant copyright-holders,
but some were unobtainable. We would be grateful if the
appropriate people could contact us.

To Des, Mario, Barry -
you were there in my heart

About the Author

Sean Mayes was born in Stone Allerton, Somerset in 1945. He left Cambridge in 1967 with a degree in philosophy and joined a rock 'n' roll band. He played piano for Fumble who toured Europe with Bill Haley and Fats Domino and in America with David Bowie in 1972. He made three LPs with Fumble and featured in the original cast of *Elvis!* at the Astoria Theatre.

In 1983 he joined Tom Robinson for 'War Baby', touring and further LP tracks.

Sean died in London in 1995.

Acknowledgements

Simon Woods, Geoff Felix, Colin Phillips, Des Henley, Mario Ferrari, Barry Pike, Chic Mayes, Rikki Beadle-Blair, Kaye and Martin Roach, Gerald Woodgate, Derek Beevor, Steve Harley, Wendy Anninson, Maggi Ronson, Kazuya, Hideaki, Youichi, Eiji and Takashi (The Yellow Monkey), and all of Sean's friends and family around the world.

Also by Sean Mayes

Kate Bush - A Visual Documentary (Omnibus Press - 1988) (with Kevin Cann)

Joan Armatrading - A Biography (Weidenfeld and Nicolson - 1990)

CONTENTS

DRAMATIS PERSONAE

David Bowie

Corrine 'Coco' Schwab – David's Personal Assistant

Pat Gibbons – David's young Manager

Tony Mascia – David's Bronx-born bodyguard and driver, died in 1991

Stu George – old friend of David's from Hull, occasional security

The Band

Carlos Alomar – guitar/musical director (wife, Robin Clarke, singer)

George Murray – bass guitar

Dennis Davis – drums

Adrian Belew – lead guitar, ex-Zappa band

Roger Powell – keyboards and synthesizers, Todd Rundgren's Utopia

Simon House – electric violin, ex-Hawkwind

Sean Mayes – piano, Fumble

Eric Barrett – tour manager, Scot living in LA

Tony Visconti – record producer, American living in London

Barbara DeWitt – public relations, LA

Tony MacGrogan – RCA London, A&R

Frank – security

Bowie Road Crew

Rob Joyce – stage manager

Moose – equipment and emergencies

Leroy – equipment and occasional bodyguard

Jan – equipment, drums

Ron – Eric's assistant, looks after travel and personnel

Showco – Sound Equipment and Lighting

Buford – sound engineer

Randy Marshall – singing roadie

Rick – piano engineer, US and Europe

Ed – piano engineer, Australia and Japan

Australia

Dennis Garcia – keyboards first three gigs

Bob and Rick – security, karate

Fumble

Des – vocals, guitar

Mario – vocals, bass

Sean – vocals, piano

Barry – drums

Jack Daniels – American bourbon whisky

INTRODUCTION

It's been four years since Sean died and I'm still surrounded by boxes of his papers, photographs and diary notes. Amongst this fascinating assortment of material are his photo albums and diary for 1978/79, a year out with David Bowie playing major concert halls around the world and recording in Switzerland.

Sean always had a book in mind when he was writing his diary. He was a prolific writer and virtually chronicled every day of his adult life, very much influenced by his grandfather, Tom Thompson, who had been a writer, broadcaster and faithful diarist. Sean was always working with 'books' in mind. It had always been his dream to write up the enormous stock-pile of amusing on-the-road incidents encountered with his group Fumble. Sean and Fumble had lived and toured together since the mid-'60s, and it was with Fumble that Sean first came into contact with David Bowie.

Bowie had seen Fumble perform on *The Old Grey Whistle Test* on BBC TV. Their timing was perfect as he was making arrangements for a forthcoming tour of America where Ziggy Stardust was starting to make serious in-roads. Fumble were booked for a few UK dates and proved that, unlike previous 'warm up' bands, they could indeed rouse an audience fit for Ziggy. The US tour followed and Fumble toured the land of their dreams, working packed theatres on one of the most significant rock tours of the '70s.

In 1978, Bowie assembled a band for all seasons, a superb Anglo-American soup of musicians which, apart from the black rhythm section, had never worked together before. Sean had had 'the call' some months before and was plucked out of a West End show where Fumble were providing the music for *Elvis!* From here on in, the diary you are about to read covers just about everything you could wish to know about life on the road with David Bowie.

So, to this book itself. A long time coming for Sean and I'm more than a little sad that he wasn't here to see it published himself. There is nothing like holding a copy of your new book for the first time, sorry it didn't happen earlier Sean.

When I began looking through the manuscript(s) again, it became clear that I wasn't just dealing with one but at least half a dozen versions of the tour diary. Over the years various edits, volumes and excerpts were made and I was left with the interesting task of compiling the version I think Sean would have liked to see himself. I also had a mountain of original tour note-books, where Sean illegibly scrawled first hand notes, together with more sensitive thoughts in a code which he had developed years earlier and which we have still to break. Having worked closely with him for at least the last seven years of his life, I believe I came to know something of his writing interests, so I approached this book with him sitting by my side, working on the same computer we bought together which still contains much of his own files for the myriad of different projects he was always working on.

I decided that I didn't just want this to be a book about his work with Bowie, that I would try and supply the reader with a slightly broader picture of what Sean was about. His story is a fascinating one, tragically cut short at 49 with AIDS in 1995, but packed full like a travelogue which was eventful right up to his death. Right up until the end he still had surprises in store, he was indeed an intriguing and complex man, but genuine and incredibly faithful to all his friends.

Kevin Cann, 1999

CHAPTER 1

REHEARSALS

March 1978

Nowadays I suppose everyone knows what Dallas is like. But in 1978 it seemed rather an unglamorous place to be rehearsing a David Bowie World Tour. I had flown out from London and checked into a smart but dull hotel on a dusty freeway fifteen miles from downtown Dallas. Just down the road was the rehearsal studio, a large windowless warehouse with a low stage at one end. Outside, the Texas sun blazed down but inside it was dark with occasional pools of light – rather like the music we were playing.

David hadn't arrived yet but Carlos Alomar was taking us through the numbers, handing out sheets of chords and singing the lead line as we strummed through. The music was a strange mixture – I had lain on my hotel bed with a cassette, listening in despair to the instrumentals on Side 2 of *"Heroes"* – I couldn't tell where one track ended and the next began! What on earth was I doing out here? But then we ran through 'Suffragette City' and I happily rocked away remembering the excitement of the '73 tours.

Back then, David was Ziggy Stardust – sassy and outrageous, the last word in decadence – and I was in the rock 'n' roll band Fumble opening the show on his American tour. We finally said "Goodbye" to David at the end of that tour in Los Angeles, but whenever I heard a Bowie record after that I sometimes wondered if he ever remembered Fumble and a piano player called Sean.

Five years later I got a phone call: "Would you like to play piano for David Bowie?" Would I just! I was still with Fumble, appearing in *Elvis!*, the West End musical, so we found another piano player to take my place for a while. I said "See you!" to Fumble and caught the plane.

Now I was sitting at a grand-piano at one side of the stage and had a good view of the rest of the band. Just near me in front of the piano was Simon House, the only other British musician – he used to be in Hawkwind. Tall, thin and *very* laid back, Simon was playing electric violin and had a look somewhere between Paganini and Keith Richards.

At the front of the stage was Carlos, singing and conducting us with sharp chops of his guitar neck. He is David's musical director and first met him when his wife Robin Clarke was doing vocals on *Young Americans* and she invited David back for dinner. He's from Puerto Rico, relaxed and friendly with a smile you could read a contract by.

On this tour, David was using his usual black rhythm section – Carlos on guitar with Dennis Davis on drums and George Murray on bass – but the rest of the band were new – Adrian Belew on lead guitar, Roger Powell on keyboards and synthesizers, Simon and me. At first I was a little nervous of the others. I thought they might snub a rock 'n' roll player, but in fact they were all as friendly as could be – no prima donnas.

Dennis is crazy and irrepressible, always joking, sometimes deadpan, possibly the original inspiration for Animal, the *Muppets* drummer. George is the complete opposite, very quiet – Lonesome George Murray as Carlos says. These three had been with David ever since 'the plastic soul' days in 1975.

At the far side of the stage were the other two 'new boys'. Adrian is from Kentucky, a slight figure. In his dungarees he looks like a farmer from a Norman Rockwell painting. David spotted him in Frank Zappa's band in Berlin and asked him to join. He has a quirky sense of humour which Zappa appreciated on-stage but not so much off.

Roger, surrounded by synthesizers, is a college graduate type – he links up computers to his keyboards and flies to Japan to demonstrate them for the manufacturers. A dry sense of humour mellows his academic personality but I think David was wary of his obvious intellect.

We were a mixed bunch but somehow got on well together. The different musical styles blended too and soon we began to feel like a band.

On Wednesday afternoon while we were rehearsing, a small group of people came into the gloom at the back of the studio, closing the door on the brilliant sunshine outside. As they approached the stage I recognised a slight, nondescript figure with fair hair and completely forgot what I was playing.

David looked tired and drawn after his 11,000 mile flight from Kenya. He had been relaxing there after filming *Just a Gigolo* in Berlin. He wore baggy trousers and a neutral short-sleeved shirt with a narrow tie, loosely knotted – "This one's from Bromley Tech!" – and looked quite ordinary compared with the last time I had seen him.

"Look," he grinned proudly, "I've got a suntan."

"You call that a tan?" drawled a Texan voice from the back of the room and we all laughed.

Though exhausted by travel, he was really excited at having a new band to play with and immediately jumped on-stage and started going through numbers. Finally Coco had to drag him away before he wrecked his voice.

Coco, *aka* Corrine Schwab, was David's constant companion – his personal assistant, wet-nurse and wardrobe mistress, who kept a very low profile with the press. Coco is small and bird-like with close-cropped hair. She is French-American, grew up all over the world including Haiti and

Switzerland and has, as you may imagine, an unplaceable accent. Her knowledge of several languages proved very useful on their travels, but so too did her natural instinct for coping with anything. She is not unflappable but her panics are good for getting things done! I believed it was more important to get on with Coco than with David and fortunately we took to each other immediately!

The next day things really got moving and the ordinary young man began to generate energy, excitement and humour. There was a chemistry about the band which was subtle but crucial and it was a great feeling as the music came together.

The atmosphere at rehearsals was not what I'd expected. Anyone watching would think Carlos was in charge and David seemed like a kid who'd been allowed to sing with the band but doesn't think the musicians are going to take him seriously. I know he is shy and got the impression that much of his joking and bounce were intended to cover his diffidence. He never told us what to do but suggested things – "How about this... Let's try that..." He was very quick to pick up on good ideas. "What was that? – it sounded great! Can you make it a bit more raunchy?"

He told me later on the tour, "I'm very suspicious of virtuosity. I like people who play with an original style and I choose people who I think can contribute something."

He allowed us great freedom and encouraged us to be creative but it was still very much his music – he seemed to direct by a process of inspiration and there was never any doubt that the final result was just what he wanted. Still he clowned, grinned, cavorted, forgot words, made up silly ones and constantly glanced at Carlos to make sure he was doing the right bit of a song. It made for a relaxed atmosphere. *Time takes a cigarette... sticks it up your arse...!*

Rehearsals were fun but exhausting. We worked solidly from 10 in the morning till 8 or 9 at night. Most tours take a month to prepare but we had only two weeks so the pressure was on.

The studio was comfortable with all the gear, a complete monitor system and a small PA. Showco was the tour company, based in Dallas, which is why we were rehearsing there. The crew was an entertaining mixture of Texans and Californians. David was rather taken with the southern accent and Adrian's all-purpose Texan exclamation, "Hell-God-Baby-Damn!" became a tour catch-phrase. We were well looked after - they'd bring food in and you only had to raise an eyebrow to get a beer or juice rushed over. After one or two near-spills I stuck a tape across the black Steinway piano with a notice NO DRINKS BEYOND THIS LINE before anything got upset into the works.

Diary Notes:

Friday 17th March: Dallas: Notes on my birthday. D down to breakfast - seems strange but of course he doesn't excite attention, dressed very conservatively. People don't know he's here. His tan is less pink and more becoming. Pushes his hair back off his face and is looking more like the old DB as he loses his tie, and dons a cream gaberdine cap.

In 'Hang On To Yourself', everyone jamming madly on the last section, he pogos to the obvious feel of the number and gives a quick grin. In 'Blackout' he starts to bop, throws a leg up in a ballet/ karate move. Everyone is moving more now anyway. The first show, it just struck us, is only twelve days away. San Diego, wow!

In the car coming across this afternoon a few of us were discussing what we would wear, and that David would look so smooth that everyone else would look ridiculous. There's a girl downtown who makes spacesuits, someone remembered…

(A few days later we made a hilarious trip there with Adrian but he decided such a suit would be too hot on-stage.)

That afternoon I came into the studio to discover three huge dark bottles of Moët & Chandon champagne on the piano standing firmly on the wrong side of the NO DRINK line. Also a shoe box tied with a mauve lurex leg warmer. The box was bulging with crazy striped socks – *A very merry birthday for Sean from Bowie 78*.

It was indeed a merry birthday. At that point we had never ventured beyond the hotel, being too tired most nights for more than a quick nightcap and sleep. But I was determined my birthday should be our first escape into downtown Dallas, and we all drove into town to a raunchy Texan rock club called Mother Blues. Drinks were on the house and we'd already polished off the champagne back at the studio. The live music was loud, so someone led us upstairs. We just found a wreck of an old dressing-room and sat around on broken chairs and burst cushions. The 'air-conditioning' was a gaping window frame through which I could see David's dark blue Lincoln limousine. Tony, his huge driver and bodyguard, stood impassively by the door, no expression on his face.

"Well," I said delightedly, "it makes a change from the hotel!"

I was amused to see David slumming it, though later I heard that this was like many of the dressing rooms on the Iggy Pop tour when David played piano for him. The drinks kept coming and later we drifted downstairs again. Fortunately I made it back to the hotel before being very sick indeed - I took Saturday's rehearsal carefully, much to David's amusement.

Tony Mascia and his limousine will be familiar to anyone who has seen *The Man Who Fell To Earth* (or *The Cat Who Fell Down*, as Dennis calls it). Tony is a true Italian from the Bronx and used to be Rocky Marciano's sparring partner. He is large and solid and I can't imagine anything getting him too excited - the ideal guy to look after our hero. He never looks truly comfortable away from his car.

Apart from my birthday, we hardly left the hotel, which stood in splendid isolation between an industrial estate and a muddy wasteland. It was a deluxe cell-block with a disco on the *n*th floor full of swinging middle-aged polyester businessmen in tired suits, served by bunny-style waitresses with fixed smiles. Breakfast apart - I *love* American breakfasts - the hotel food was dull and not cheap. The hotel motto was 'We know what you want' and I imagined this chanted by a seedy garden gnome with plastic wings. You were encouraged to feel about as individual as an inflight meal.

My room was large and comfortable though and I tried to make it feel like home. This meant papers everywhere and the typewriter in the middle of it all. I put my 'Good Luck' cards from home on the TV, covered the ghastly wall picture with an Elvis poster and played classical cassettes late at night. On my sixth floor balcony I put a plastic trash can full of ice and imported beers. I did miss my cat.

Dallas itself is a typical southern city, a background of bleached desert tones scrawled over with neon. Mostly long, low buildings on wide dusty roads where every customised fast food establishment glows like a giant's toy in the splendour of its own parking lot. At the centre of this sprawling grid the downtown pile of sharp office blocks juts like a designer mountain of glass and concrete. In 1978, I somehow couldn't see the glamour of Dallas!

I did love the cars, though. During the rehearsal period we were ferried between hotel and studio in beat-up old hire cars, but they were still large and American with spongy suspensions, the metal hot and burnished under the Texas sun.

One day, early on, David said, "Let's do the whole of the *Ziggy Stardust* album - that'll surprise them!"

We finally settled on six numbers but only after learning the whole lot. It was a strange experience for me - like a time warp back to 1973. Once when he sang *I'm a space invader!* he turned towards us with his fingers circling his eyes - the Martian goggles. "*Freak out in a moonage daydream, oh yeah...* Do you remember that?" he called as the number finished.

I remembered only too well the monster who once mesmerised us all and held me very much in awe when Fumble were touring with him. His appearance then was bizarre even off-stage. His white skin had a waxy translucence and his eyebrows were plucked right off. He looked as if the blood had fled his face into that alien hair. His clothes were that pre-punk style he created with a sidelong glance at the '50s - tight fitting, black and savage colours, more plastic than glitter - the glitter was in his eyes, unnaturally bright.

"I never thought I'd be singing *Hey man!* along with you on-stage one day," I said.

"I never thought *I'd* be doing Ziggy in 78!" said David with a grin.

When Adrian was working on the solo to 'Hang on' Simon remarked that it reminded him of the trombone theme to the old radio series *Hancock's Half Hour*. David laughed and said that tune had in fact inspired him!

We had one break from the heavy schedule on the evening when they first screened *The Rutles* (the Beatles spoof). We were all keen to see it as almost every one of us owed his original impulse to pick up a guitar to the Fab Four. We finished early that night and rushed back to the hotel. Then David phoned me.

"Do you want to come up to my suite and watch the programme with me and Coco?"

At times like this you forget you've been working all day with the guy and I felt thrilled at the honour! But, of course, he was ringing round inviting everyone and his room was soon full of the group plus one or two wives, girlfriends and even a baby.

We all fell about over the programme and David had fun imagining how John (Lennon) would react.

"I'm sure he's watching it but he'll probably pretend he didn't bother!" David's loud laugh still echoes his Cockney youth. "Let's get the LP and use it as the intro music for the show."

So we were soon to be jumping around back-stage singing *Hold my hand, yeah yeah!* getting in the mood to go on-stage.

Towards the end of rehearsals, David's voice gave out and we spent the last few days running through the complete set while the lighting crew got the hang of the show. Everyone was getting nervous and we were far from note-perfect, but finally the time ran out. On Saturday, 25th March, two weeks after I'd arrived in Dallas, three huge trucks of gear were driving west across the desert headed for San Diego, our first gig.

That night we all went out to a bowling alley, a huge place with twenty lanes, plus bars, pool tables, etc. We were in a lively mood and kept shouting to each other to watch the TV where they were showing old Ed Sullivan Show specials including classic snatches of Presley and the Beatles.

Later some of us moved to the pool tables. I went to the bar to order some beers and the barman wondered if I was from England.

"What are you doing over here?" he asked, just to be friendly.

I hesitated a moment then muttered something about holidays and travelling. I suddenly realised that if I told him what I was really doing I'd break the spell of that free evening. There was David chalking a cue and asking the young guy at the next table something about the rules, and no one dreamed who he was. Then it was brought home to me just how precious moments like this must be to someone of his status and how much I should hate to give up such simple pleasures myself. Fame!

When David sat down later, he tucked one leg up under him and I noticed that the sole of his shoe was as clean as the day he'd bought it. OK, maybe the shoes were new, but it struck me that he hardly ever sets foot in the street. It's all hotels, limousines, sterilised airports – the life I was about to lead. I shivered, feeling poised at the top of a rollercoaster about to sweep across the world.

CHAPTER 2

FIRST NIGHT

Monday, 27th March

The Monday after rehearsals we flew out of Dallas. The rough old hire-cars took us to the airport, we had a few drinks then took off across the desert for San Diego on the west coast. Our descent was spectacular. We plunged into a lake of white cloud from which tree-covered mountain tops rose like mysterious islands and outside the portholes everything went white. Suddenly we emerged through the ceiling of cloud, flying very low over the sparkling city - coastal resort and naval base. The airport lights marked out its perimeter in the waters of the Pacific Ocean.

I was still in a daze as we were led through the busy airport terminal full of flustered Mexicans and fresh young servicemen in white caps, belts and gaiters. Outside lining the sidewalk were three long black Cadillac limousines and David's dark blue Lincoln. We cruised between palm trees on to Harbor Island and stepped out on the crescent drive in front of our glorious hotel.

I had a beautiful, large yellow room. I put my bag down and slid aside the full length window to step onto the balcony overlooking the glittering yacht marina. On one or two of the deluxe floating apartments I could see the dull red glow of a barbecue. I made a trip to the ice machine down the corridor then stood sipping a Jack Daniels bourbon and breathing the warm ocean air. This was rock 'n' roll!

We all met up in the lounge bar overlooking the sea. David was in very buoyant mood and I was exhilarated to be 6000 miles from home and on the brink. The lounge band didn't seem so excited though.

Tuesday was hot and sunny, revealing blue sea and palm trees. I breakfasted downstairs on fresh pineapple in the coffee shop overlooking the Pacific. This is California!

Later I took a cab downtown and stepped out onto the sidewalk, camera swinging. I found myself opposite a small dark shop with an attractive girl sitting outside. She called me over.

"Hi – do you want to come in for a rap?"

A rap? A wrap? A federal rap?

"What's that?" I asked.

"Come on," she said, "is there anything you want to talk to me about?"

"That's all right, honey," I said shaking my head and strolled on up the road.

Soon I found myself on a sleazy side street with a few cheap clothes shops, bars and plenty of boarded-up windows. A cop car screeched to a rocking halt just behind me. They jumped out and ran into one of the doorways. America is just like the movies! A small crowd gathered but nothing happened.

Soon I ran into Simon and Dennis who were heading for a music shop. The guy there welcomed Dennis as an old friend and invited him to try a new drum kit, so he stormed his way around it.

Back at the hotel, everyone was feeling restless and beginning to get edgy. Somehow the prospect of another twenty four hours without playing was unbearable. We wandered between each others' rooms - television, music, a few drinks, a little smoking - no one could settle to anything. Down in the bar, I chatted to Natasha Kornilof, a small and homely figure who designed David's stage clothes and was making last minute alterations. Tony Mascia told us how the sewing machine had been delivered to his room and the small, fussy man had insisted on explaining how to use it - until Tony gently placed him outside the door. He spread his massive hands, "What do I want to know about one of them things for?"

17

Wednesday kicked off with excitement turning to nervousness as the day progressed. At 4pm we left for the sound-check. I clambered into the limo clutching plastic bags of stage clothes and got my cheap camera ready to snap our first stadium... then suddenly there it was - the vast, almost sinister concrete oval looming across the deserted parking lot. At the back-stage entrance there were a couple of security guards on the gate and a few kids hanging over the railings. The cars nosed their way down the steep ramp while the steel shutter-door wound slowly up. We drove into the gloom of the building and the door closed behind us, a modern portcullis. I headed straight for the arena, bags and all, and hurried up the steps onto the stage to survey the 15,000 empty waiting seats. It was breathtaking and I gaped.

I walked out into the auditorium to get a fan's-eye view of the stage: a five-foot platform of scaffolding with a floor of shiny black plexiglass. The backdrop was a sixteen foot fence of white neon tubes. Above and on both sides was suspended a gantry of lights so we would be playing in a cage of black metal and white light, all reflected in the ebony mirror floor. The structure looked vaguely sinister.

We took a long time getting the sound and monitors right, while an army of road crew clambered about on the gantry illuminating us from every direction.

Eric was in charge now - he was the tour manager, an emigré Scot who lived in Los Angeles. He was responsible for every facet of touring – the technical side and the welfare of musicians and road crew. Some tour managers treat the star as God and everyone else can go hang, but Eric looked after everyone and had everyone's respect. He even told David what to do – politely!

So we retired to the dressing-rooms – concrete, windowless and ugly with a lingering locker-room aroma. But for today they are transformed, furnished with carpets, chairs and long tables spread with a cold buffet and baskets of fruit and flowers. There were large ice-bins of beers and soft drinks, and bottles of wine and spirits – Chevas Regal, Jack Daniels, Remy Martin and Stolichnaya. We would need to go gently before the show!

Eric had an assistant, Ron, a young American who had the unenviable task of looking after fifteen untogether people – hotel to gig to airport. He told us the procedure for leaving the stadium after the show.

It was funny to see everyone getting ready for the show – seven guys and seven different images. George's black and white Japanese kimono, (sometimes he wore a long jacket and cowboy hat, visible in silhouette next to David's elbow on the cover of *Stage*). Adrian's Hawaiian shirts, my punk/'50s look and Dennis wearing anything that came into his head. Carlos started the tour in elegant mauve velvet, but by Australia he was looking almost as punk as me! David had his own dressing-room with a long mirror and Coco busy at the ironing board, but he wandered in to chat to us. He always dreams up some new look and appeared that first night in a green PVC lounge suit and a small smile that seemed to say, "I know it's ridiculous but I dare you to laugh!"

Eric had been shouting the time to us, "18 minutes! ...11 minutes! ...3 minutes, you guys!" and now herded us out of the dressing-room towards the stage. Then, "Wait here!" and we were just around the corner from the entrance and could hear the crowd. We were all nervous but excited.

"How's your voice?"

"Oh, it should be fine now I've rested it."

I hate waiting to go on and started to pogo to release the tension. A moment later we were all jumping up and down and laughing, feeling much better. Then "Let's go!" shouted Eric and we walked around the corner in a loose bunch, David among us. The house lights were still up, stage lights down. A few people saw us, there were a few shouts, but no one thought it was starting yet because of the lights. Then they spotted him, realised this was it and the shouts spread to a roar of 15,000, a thunder of welcoming noise.

The stage was polished like glass and I felt I had forgotten how to walk, how to put one foot in front of the other. I thought I might fall over before I reached the piano. Carlos picked up his baton and walked to the front of the stage. He turned to face us. David stood at his keyboard and watched Carlos calmly. Carlos raised his arms, began the count... *BOOM!* The first sombre note of 'Warsawa' rang out and the crowd roared. *BOOM!* There was a glow from the lights around the stage. *BOOM!* The auditorium started to dim. *BOOM!* Darkness beyond the edge of the stage – another roar. *BOOM!* My eyes were watering now as the lights blazed – it was like staring at the sun. The theme started like a church organ. David had a quizzical look on his face. Carlos beamed. David grinned back then looked across to me. I felt my heart would burst. The music swelled then came to a pause, David took the mike and *Sula vi... deleo* echoed around the vast stadium. A roar shook the place. Simon's eerie violin screeched out the responses. The instrumental paced steadily on. The tension in the place was palpable. Then the last few measured notes... a pause... One, two, three, "HEROES"! A frenzy burst over the crowd, people were jumping to their feet, waving their arms wildly. "He's back! He's back! We love you!"

There is something miraculous about first nights. The things you always got wrong in rehearsals come out right, unexpected mistakes go unnoticed, a joyous fear carries you through.

'What In The World' – the first half of this was now a limping reggae beat. We had been fooling around at rehearsals one day waiting for David, when he arrived and liked it so it stayed. The last verse was at full tilt and the lights blazed again, showing up scores of faces down in front of us. More relaxed now, I started to scan for foxes (good-lookers) and anything crazy or funny - the different images, the look-alikes.

I soon noticed something eerie - hundreds of pairs of large, round pale discs of light gazing down from the sides of the bowl... binoculars were *de rigeur* at these big American concerts but I simply thought: *Diamond Dogs*! It was as if some strange creatures were peering out of caves in the walls.

I won't go right through that first night, I was concentrating so hard most of it didn't register.

'Fame' was David's biggest hit in the States and it finished the first half.

"We'll be back in ten short minutes," he lied, and with a wave we all disappeared back-stage, talking our heads off to anyone around, grabbing a drink, exulting. Twenty minutes later we walked out again, this time with the house lights down. Dennis started the limping drum beat of 'Five Years' (something he never quite got right!) and there were shouts and cheers though it was hard to tell if anyone recognised it. Then David appeared to an ecstatic welcome - snakeskin drapecoat and huge baggy white pants. David, you look ridiculous and I love you!

"I'd like to introduce my band... Sean Mayes on piano!"

Careful not to trip over leads, I ran to the front of the stage and gave a thumbs up to the invisible crowd, a broad grin on my face.

"Simon House on violin!" who bowed coolly with a small smile.

So he continued through the band then we crashed out the first chord – THRUM... *Pushing through the market square*... delight from 15,000... *Five years*... people were holding up five spread fingers, mouthing the words.

Then the bombshells followed – 'Soul love'! 'Star'! David dancing, bouncing, kicking – this is not Bowie posing, it's David having a ball. 'Hang On To Yourself'! The neons spill daylight across the jumping crowd. *Ziggy played guitar*... a roar for this anthem. 'Suffragette City'... and there's electric expectancy until *Aaaah... Wham, Bam, Thank you Ma'am!* as the crowd leapt to its feet shouting.

Tonight and on most of the American tour he played 'Rock 'n' roll Suicide' and as the lights came up there he was with a cigarette in his hand, a souvenir of conceits of the past.

"What on earth can I do after Ziggy?" he had wondered one day at rehearsal.

"Have to be something to bring the energy right down – you can't top it," I said "How about 'Art Decade'?" And 'Art Decade' it now was with the strange coloured spotlights swinging round to discover the crowd. As they realised he could see them they jumped up, waving, hoping to catch his eye and a gentle little instrumental turned into a near-riot.

Then followed 'Station to Station', Roger's steam engine so realistic you could almost see the steam and smell the sulphur. The song built with strong piston strokes, up and up until – *It's not the side effect of the cocaine – I'm thinking that it must be love*! It is love. Every light opens up – spotlights stab, floods blaze, neon glares – white out! It nearly lifts me from my seat. *It's too late!* It is – it's a landslide. *It's too late!* No wonder he wanted a rock 'n' roll piano player. *The European cannon is here...* is David the European cannon? Who cares – David is here. The final romp, over and over, not wanting it ever to end. *The return of the thin white duke, making pure white stains.* The guitar pizzicato, pure '50s, tiptoes out – a quick bow and we're running off.

Back for a double encore, 'TVC15' and 'Stay', finishing with an ecstatic, bouncing 'Rebel Rebel', David camp in his sailor's cap, grinning broadly. The bouncers have given up the task of keeping everyone from the barriers and now it's just a sea of people on their feet, on other people's feet, on chairs, on shoulders, waving arms, throwing flowers, scarves... he catches one bunch of roses and the crowd somehow manage to raise a cheer above the rest.

Suddenly it's over, we run off. The limos are waiting in a line, doors open, engines purring. Ron shouts – "Sean in here – Carlos there – where's George?" The steel shutter is rolling up, the cars surge forward, a few cops keep the kids outside from making human sacrifices, and we're zig-zagging fast through the packed parking lot, escaping before the 15,000. More police halt traffic while we swing out on to the main road, then we're cruising back to the hotel.

"Any beers back there? Someone got an opener? God, turn the heat off! Hi sweetheart! Anyone seen my jacket?"

In the hotel bar David was ecstatic, hugging us and bubbling over with delight. The show had been a success and after the tension of the past few days, we all felt a surge of joy. The lobby was full of fans and they gradually infiltrated the bar. David sat in a corner with the rest of us around him as a buffer. The kids came up in ones and twos for autographs and to say how knocked out they were with the show.

Now imagine the scene – a posh lounge bar full of businessmen and elderly vacationers, on-stage the cabaret band making a polite sound behind the conversation. Then Dennis came over and said it was OK with the band if we wanted to jam on their gear... The next twenty minutes proved that some of us were rockers, others raised on funk and all of us well-oiled. After a few false starts we played the only music we all knew – Bowie songs, ones we had learned but dropped before the show – 'Sound And Vision' etc. During one solo, David sat down on-stage and smiled at the audience who just stared from behind their tables. The fans at the back must have been flipping to see David let his hair down but the worthies in front of us didn't even recognise him! Soon we all fled giggling to our corner and the musak returned. Amazingly our pub-rock gig got a friendly review next day in *The Los Angeles Times*!

I can remember little of our early departure the next

morning which is hardly surprising. We flew over a strange desert landscape scored by straight white roads which seemed to form a geometric pattern and lead nowhere. Phoenix, Arizona, welcomed us with hot sunshine and the gig went well. We had the next day free and lazed around the hotel pool. David, who wishes he could swim like a dolphin, cannot swim at all but lay there in dark glasses and turquoise trunks improving his tan while a handful of fans huddled bug-eyed behind the fence.

That evening, to my surprise, we were able to saunter out of the hotel and walk down the road to a Japanese restaurant. We were on the outskirts of town and the road was quiet, the sky very dark and distant. We seemed to be out of time and place – two days into a world tour and we could step aside for an evening.

The restaurant was traditional and we removed our shoes at the door and sat on the floor at a long, low table. I had never tasted Japanese food before but David ordered the unusual delicacies (raw fish, seaweed) for those of us with the courage to try. He told us about Japan, a place he loves. He takes holidays there but has only toured once, in 1973.

When we left, David thanked the kimonoed waitresses and they laughed with high, tinkling voices behind delicate hands. One or two shyly requested autographs. We shall be in Japan in December and I try to imagine it as we walk back under the palm trees.

Fresno is a large industrial town in California – not my

image of that sunshine state. This was the gig where we shook out all our mistakes - and left them there! But Los Angeles was waiting.

CHAPTER 3

WEST COAST

Monday, 3rd April

I caught a glimpse of the ocean as we flew down over green hills and canyons into Los Angeles. Soon buildings were flashing past our wing-tips and the plane bumped gently down on the hot tarmac. We emerged into dazzling sunshine, palm trees shading the sidewalk, and everyone was in good spirits as the limos cruised across the city to Hollywood – and they really do cruise on the wide LA boulevards.

Hollywood is not a giant film set, as I used to imagine, but the central area of Los Angeles where the film studios are based. Sunset Boulevard runs right through it for miles till it meets the ocean. Our hotel was on a steep hill just off the Boulevard - a bright white two-storey building with a striped awning almost lost in lush tropical vegetation.

The hotel suites formed a square around the swimming-pool edged with plastic grass. I unpacked and made a few phone calls trying to track down friends, then we were off to the gig.

The Forum is a huge sports auditorium – 19,000 and very impressive. A TV crew arrived for a brief interview with David. As we walked the long route to the stage, they scuffled backwards before him and the rest of us jostled cheerfully for camera angles. Then Eric gave the shout, cameras were forgotten and we strolled out to mount the scaffolding of our first real biggie. I felt as if my heart was pumping pure adrenalin round my system and it was an effort to breathe. The audience must have felt the same way as 'Warsawa' boomed round this space age forum.

Back in 1973, the crowds at smaller gigs were always full of freaks, red-headed and otherwise. Today, the thousands who come are mostly regular rock fans with just a sprinkling of 'wowies'. But some places still celebrate and Los Angeles is one of them – at least the camp followers made good 'n' sure they got seats at the front. There was a heady feeling of celebrity facing celebrity with the show being staged on both sides of the footlights – David Bowie meets Los Angeles at The Forum.

After the show, another surging get-away, then we took a couple of limos over to The Rainbow Club on Sunset Strip, not far from the hotel. This was a place to see and be seen, but nice and casual. We marched in under the gaze of the girl on the door. She has seen it all and you can read anything into that gaze – awe, boredom, greed, fatigue, even welcome? We headed straight for a large round corner table and set up court while a hundred divine close friends came to pay homage – and in LA everyone has at some time met, spoken to, been to bed with, been at a party with, or knows a friend of, David and every other star.

"Loved the show, David…" "Hi David, what have you been up to…" "Jimmy sends his love…" "Darling, you're looking marvellous…" Lethal smiles like laser beams are flashed from one close friend to another.

I took a wander about the club looking for talent. The people standing about watched me coolly, looked very unapproachable – as I expect I did myself. You know, I have a theory that most cool crowds are composed of shy, lonely people who steel themselves to run the gauntlet of the city's top clubs and daren't smile at anyone. Just recently I was in a fashionable London club: David was standing at the bottom of the stairs and people nodded to him as they passed. When we left one kid came running out after us along the pavement. "David, please can I have your autograph? I couldn't ask you in there." Then he kissed him and ran off, as excited as any schoolboy.

Back in The Rainbow, the lights finally went up as the place was closing and everyone stood up to go. People were still rushing up to say their bit, delaying our departure, as I stood on the edge of the throng.

"Hey, who are they making all the fuss about over there?" A slight brunette called Anna was standing beside me looking up with large dark eyes. She wore a slinky but unsensational soft patterned dress and a black wool shawl about her shoulders, Spanish style. I explained who all the fuss was about.

"Oh, I just looked in to find my girlfriend – I didn't know he was here." She looked at the fair head within the scrum. "I don't know how all those people can just go up and try to talk to him."

"Most of them seem to know him."

"Oh, do you know him?"

"Yes – I play piano in the band."

We chatted for a few minutes until everyone drifted outside. Anna didn't spot her friend till we were sitting in the limo. Most of the crowd were hanging around outside looking lost. We drew alongside a particularly garish blonde in tight pink satin pants and the window hummed open. "Do you want to come back for a party?" But she didn't – she looked at the Cadillac as if it was a cattle truck. So the window hummed up and the car slid on to Sunset Strip. There was no party when we got back. Anna and I said "goodnight" to the others and chatted over bourbon till we fell asleep.

Next day we breakfasted on waffles with syrup and ice-cream down on Santa Monica.

★ ★ ★

In the middle of our LA week, we flew up to San Francisco for a show. On the plane, a young woman in tweed suit and glasses leaned across the aisle to ask me if that was David Bowie travelling first class. We got talking. The lady, Carol, ran a photographic studio in San Francisco with her friend Charles. She said I could phone her after the gig and they could show me something of the city.

We stayed at the Hyatt Regency down by the harbour. The architect had certainly had fun. It was a vast hollow pyramid, three sides that met in a point thirty storeys above our heads. Instead of corridors there were open galleries linking the rooms on each floor. The elevators were glass-sided and zipped up the wall on open tracks. I stepped out shakily on the fifteenth floor. Far below was a restaurant open to the vault with a lamp hanging from the roof on a 29-storey cable!

I retreated into the room which was to be mine for the next eighteen hours – twin double-beds, a sea of thick, soft, wall-to-wall, a view of modern towers and ancient roofs. I found some jazz on the radio and stripped off to shower away the flight with hotel soap, shampoo, bath scent, face-flannel and an acre of matching bath towel.

I went out for postcards and razor-blades and was tempted to jump on a cable car climbing one of those San Francisco hills, but we soon had to leave for the gig.

We nosed on to a flyover rising to circle a couple of 'scrapers and headed out over the bay on a mile of multi-storey bridge bound for Oakland Coliseum.

On a long tour your memory of individual gigs becomes blurred but certain things stand out. In "Heroes" David soon started to hit a new high note in the fourth verse - deadpan delivery jumps an octave - *And I, I would be king... and YOU! would be my queen.* You can hear this on *Stage* and every time it would give me a lift. When he didn't sing it, I felt cheated.

When we got back after the show, Coco called me to say David was inviting everyone to a Japanese restaurant and could they all meet in my room? I ran around the vault to the ice-machine and twenty minutes later most of the group were sitting around sipping bourbon or beer while David was looking through a photo album. For years on the road with Fumble I always carried a cheap 35mm camera and now had a 'Best of...' album including a few from David's '73 tour.

The photographers Carol and Charles arrived and I gave them drinks. I had asked David if a couple of friends could come along. Everything was relaxed until Charles produced a camera.

"Hey David, I'm a freelance photographer and I wonder if I could take a few shots of you..."

David groaned "Oh, no" and put his head in his hands. Coco jumped up between him and the offending weapon. Tony looked coolly in Charles' direction. I wanted to die.

Perhaps I was taken for a fool – it was certainly careless not to tell them, "Don't bring a camera." Charles appeared hurt by David's refusal, "You shouldn't cut yourself off from people like this!" Before things went any further I had to do something. Having invited them I should look after them so as the others got up to go I said to go on without me and tried to explain to my two guests why DB & Co. sometimes freak out at the sight of a camera.

So the three of us went to a cheap Chinese restaurant with a crazy waiter. Charles explained that he was always taking photos and did so throughout the meal. When we came out it was pouring with rain, water gushing down the steep streets. I was wearing sandals so my striped birthday socks were soon soaked.

At the airport next day I apologised to David over breakfast.

"I thought they looked a bit predatory," he commented.

"I knew something was up when I saw her talking to you on the plane," said Coco.

"Oh well, I'll know next time," I said ruefully.

On Friday, Eric had a party at his house. Anna came round and we drove out of Hollywood up through a canyon. The steep road wound between banks of lush tropical vegetation, the heavy limousine settling into each hairpin bend like a steamer into a trough. We caught glimpses of the extraordinary homes which eccentric people have built over the decades – villas, palaces, cabins, churches, Spanish, Greek, Moorish, delights and monstrosities, smart and shabby, dazzling and derelict.

We climbed out of the soft depths of the car to breathe the scented air. The lowering afternoon sun glowed on a green garden which seemed on loan from the jungle, and a comfortable house clung to the side of the hill.

It was a real treat to be in someone's home, not a hotel. We met Chris, Eric's lady, a golden-haired Californian. There was a smoking barbecue and tubs of iced beers, everything pleasantly relaxed. Later we all crowded into a back room with David to watch the TV spot from The Forum. On-stage they showed 'Jean Genie' (I suppose they always will) and I was interested to see how much David projected to the front, which I wasn't aware of behind my piano.

Then we wandered about, perused Eric's collection of souvenirs - gold discs of Jim Hendrix, Linda Ronstadt, James Taylor and David and some striking live photos.

Later Anna had to go, so we rode down in one of the waiting cars. Coming back up I sat in front with Jason the driver, clean-cut in his uniform. He told me he had studied philosophy before his chauffeur job, which is funny because I took philosophy before joining a group. In his quiet way he seemed to be a character you would only meet in America - not typical but truly American. I found his politeness strange and put it down to a professional manner but looking back I feel that may have been the way he was.

Back at Eric's, Jason stayed in the car and declined even a

soft drink. I headed back into the party where I met my friend Art, whom I knew from 1973 when Fumble supported David on his US tour. A rock 'n' roll freak, Art was delighted at a '50s band turning up with the record company he worked for. As he and I are both typewriter bashers we have managed to stay in touch. It was good to see him again and catch up on news from the past few years. Eric appeared, "Hey there, guys, everything OK? Want to join me in a vodka?" He produced a bottle of one hundred per cent proof, frosted and smoking from the freezer and poured us each a fierce slug which burned all the way down.

Later we roared down the canyon in Art's VW Beetle and went to a couple of bars. I enjoyed ligging about in LA, swigging beers, chatting to one or two friends of his. He just introduced me as a guy from an English band. I was surprised at first but realised it made sense. I've since learned it's better not to mention the Bowie connection first thing on meeting someone or the conversation always hits the same groove.

As he drove me back to the hotel I said, "You know, I feel strange being in a top band. It's funny how these things happen." He told me how he used to be chummy with Bob Dylan (they both liked Jerry Lee Lewis). One night Bob told him, "I'm putting a new band together – know any good guitarists?" "What an opportunity to do someone a favour", Art said, "but I just couldn't think of anyone at the time!"

Next morning we had breakfast in a little roadside café, a Californian concoction of eggs, crispy bacon, fresh fruit and salad, then went to a couple of garage sales. LA is a collector's paradise – clothes, cars, bikes, furniture, records, kitsch – you can pick up a chunk of the American Dream for a few dollars. Then it was time to join the excursion. Into the limos, on to the plane, off to Houston, Texas, and the south.

CHAPTER 4

SOUTHERN STATES

Saturday, 8th April

The five-hour flight continued our North American slog, eighteen cities in four weeks across the States and Canada, ending in New York.

Houston is America's fastest growing city, near Galveston on the coast and the space base up the road. We arrived early evening at another Hyatt extravaganza - three-storey lobby and lighting by Damocles.

It was Saturday night and free so we asked the staff about the best clubs and hired a limo to go visit them - Carlos, myself and a couple of the crew. The first place didn't like the way we were dressed. After that they were too smart, too rough, wanted ID, looked like clip joints or closed last month. We ended up back at the hotel with a couple of six-packs and a bag of potato chips. Next day I found out Lou Reed had been playing in town and had a party afterwards at the hotel!

The show next day went well, an 18,000 seater. However, they had four huge video screens up in the dome, which I found distracting and never quite got off on the show.

After the gig I cleaned off my make-up, showered and had a beer. As I dropped to ground level in a glass bubble elevator, I was still slightly irritable. There was a crowd of fans in the lobby standing around or sitting in the sunken cocktail bar. Simon was talking to a couple of eye-catchers, a blonde in a black lace corset and a brunette in a shiny silver spacesuit. They waved to me.

"Hi - it's the piano player! - are you Sean?" (I think she said "Seen" which always bugs me). "What shall we do? Where do you wanna go?"

Searching for a quick put-down I said, "Where's the best gay club in town?"

"Oh, that's that old Plantation - we were going to take you all there. Everyone goes to The Plantation."

I had a puzzled beer while they sorted out transport. Half the lobby squeezed into three cars and off we went.

The Plantation was a large, ranch-style place, very friendly. Drinks were cheap and the club was buzzing, plenty of jeans and cowboy boots, a few people dressed up. There was a drag act on-stage, four guys doing the Pointer Sisters, tacky but fun. Most of the people had been to the gig - "Nice show, guys!" - but no hysterics. Kathy - silver suit - told me that down south all the kids go to gay clubs as the atmosphere isn't heavy like the straight places. This was certainly relaxed and I thought David and Coco might like to come over.

I tried to ring them but ran into problems, of course. I didn't know their room number and it's no good saying breezily, "Hi, I'm in the band - could you put me through to Mr. Bowie?" So I tried calling Frank, the security guy. He wasn't in his room so I left a message with the operator. Next morning Coco told me I had started a minor panic - "David thought you'd got into some kind of trouble and called Frank to come and rescue you!"

Anyway, back at the ranch we went back-stage and met the boys who looked rather plain without their glad rags. Later, I asked Kathy if she would come back for the night. When we dropped Linda off, she insisted on getting her camera and a faulty flash to have a picture with me. She could hardly stand and broke off every now and then to lie on the grass and laugh. We were all fairly giggly by this stage but Kathy and I made it back to the hotel and negotiated the Apollo elevator without incident.

I had a 9 o'clock call next morning - a drizzly Monday. Fortunately, Kathy's outfit was reversible to black so she didn't have to face the rush hour in a silver space-suit! I had a bad hangover and grabbed a V8 (tomato juice) in the coffee shop under the hanging light. I felt better at the airport after steak and eggs and some great reviews.

We flew into Dallas again and drove in from DFW airport, past our old rehearsals hotel. This time we were staying at the plush and classic Fairmont. Even the sand in the ashtrays was monogrammed – molded into the letter F. The rooms were cold though, as we were taking bad weather on tour with us.

There were several familiar faces back-stage at the Convention Centre and there was a party atmosphere as it was Pat's birthday. Pat Gibbons was David's business manager, looking like an American college kid but with the quiet assurance of one whose father has just endowed the college with a library. He used to promote concerts at the Tower Theatre, Philadelphia when he was 22 and remembered Fumble's birthday party for George Washington in 1973. But tonight was his birthday so the local caterer who had looked after us during rehearsals had made him a huge cake. A shy Pat, who's not used to being the star himself, had to blow out all the candles.

That night's show went really well – the first one where we all settled in and just enjoyed ourselves. Four numbers were filmed for TV and later shown on the *Whistle Test*.

Back at the hotel, David invited us all for supper in the Venetian Room, the hotel's restaurant. We had a couple of long tables near the stage and wine and seafood started to arrive. We toasted Pat and his wife Peggy and I gave him a Snoopy card with some reference to Beauty and the Beast, then the lights went down and a band took to the stage. Billy

Davis and Marilyn McCoo were appearing and their band came on first to play a few numbers. I nudged Coco, "Hey, look at that piano player!" The lights were down but I sensed something special about the dark figure who took command of the stage. Black, short-haired, plumpish, in a tight tuxedo, striking face but... was it a guy or a girl? The lights went up on-stage and we decided it was a woman. ("Hey David," Coco whispered across the table, "look at the piano player!") She was fascinating, counting the band into each number, playing with great style then jumping up to conduct the last bars for a tight finish.

The stars came on and were very good but we were mostly watching the piano player. At one point Billy Davis said, "Ladies and gentlemen, we have a star with us here tonight!" and David stood up with a slight smile and bent his head to the applause. In a funny way, I felt proud of him but almost protective, aware that to most of the people in the room he was just a name and the applause was polite.

The kids outside knew just who he was though – quite a crowd had collected behind the red curtained entrance. In due course, David made his escape through a service exit so they had to make do with the rest of us when we emerged.

In the bar, I spotted the piano player and introduced myself. She was Gayle Dietrich, living in LA. She was planning a solo career and I wished her luck. I must confess I tried to buy some flowers to send up later but everything was closed.

After last night I felt shattered when I crawled out of the elevator and someone had stubbed a cigar out in the monogrammed sand.

★ ★ ★

Baton Rouge – the name has a ring to it, right down there on the Mississippi, but we flew in over one of the filthiest industrial estates I've ever seen. The airport and hotel were right out in the green though and everything was awash with rain.

The LSU Assembly Centre looks like a large flying saucer has just landed. It holds 11,000 people and the sheriff's police had them well under control. This was a drag at first but they got excited by the end of the show.

Afterwards I met a few kids in the hotel lobby, then David arrived with Coco and Frank. They wanted to go for something to eat so the kids told us of a club nearby and eagerly piled into cars to go there themselves. Somehow in the rush, the four of us got left behind! David decided he'd rather walk – we could see the club but it turned out to be on the other side of the freeway and there were a few cars rushing out of the night. We persuaded David not to make a dash for it – I had a dreadful vision of our hero breathing his last on a Louisiana freeway – and we squeezed into another car. David and the others had a meal while I chatted with a table of kids. Later, David spent most of his time signing autographs and answering questions. I generally steer clear of him at times like this but some fans still wonder how I can avoid his company for even a minute.

CHAPTER 5

MID-WEST

Wednesday, 12th April

Next day we flew to Nashville via Atlanta. We stayed in a shabby Hilton hotel on the wrong side of the river. The grubby picture-window didn't open, the air-conditioning unit sounded like traffic. There was a faint chemical smell.

Adrian's home was just outside Nashville but so many friends were in town for the show that he lent them his house while his wife and baby daughter moved into his hotel room. We were free that night so Adrian suggested Fanny's, the rock club where Zappa had discovered him playing with a local band. Carlos, Simon and I found a few of the road crew there knocking back beers. The three of us went over the road to a tiny diner for tuna fish 'n' cheddar sandwiches. I stuck some rock 'n' roll on the juke box and we chatted to the waitress – it felt good just to get away from endless hotels.

Back at Fanny's, I got the names of a couple of gay clubs from the guys on the door. Carlos decided to come along too. He's not gay but often likes the ambience. The Cabaret was another ranch-style place, loud disco, few people but it seemed to suit our mood. We ordered a couple of beers and I noticed a tall, attractive youth leaning against the bar. Carlos and I sat at a table and watched the dancers. He was in a good mood – as always! I told him he should be careful with that smile of his. "It'll get you into trouble one of these nights," I said.

"That's all right," he smiled, "I'm not worried!"

The youth I had noticed had a dance with a guy then returned to the bar alone. I decided to move in quickly. I went up to the bar for another beer, then turned to him. He met my gaze.

"Hi," I said, nervous but confident.

"Hello."

"Are you going to the Bowie concert tomorrow?"

"No."

"Do you want to? I'm in the band."

"You're kidding!" But he believed me, he was a dancer. "I'm not doing anything much right now. I've just been to Florida for a few weeks."

He had a southern drawl which was attractive and I had to stop myself grinning. I asked him how old he was.

"Eighteen."

"Oh."

"That's OK, I'm legal!"

Matthew and I sat down with Carlos. We ordered some more beers and he asked me if I wanted to dance. As I've two left feet and hate disco music and he was a professional dancer I wasn't keen, but Carlos was, so soon they were both gyrating to the loud and funky music.

Later Matthew drove us back to the hotel,

"My Ma let me have the car tonight."

"Does she know where you take it?"

"Yeah, she knows. She doesn't mind. So long as I get back in time for her to drive to work."

Next morning I woke at eight with the sun viciously stabbing between the curtains. I woke Matthew who was horrified at the time. He grabbed his clothes while I crawled back into bed.

Woke again later still feeling wrecked. That afternoon Simon and I took a cab into town as his violin bow needed repairing. We found a fascinating workshop, benches strewn with pieces of saxophones, guitars, unidentified chunks of wood and metal projecting from clamps. Then we went to Broadway to look for clothes.

They call Nashville 'Music City, USA'. Broadway is Music Street, wide and dusty with square old buildings and everything faded in the sun. It's lined with music stores, small bars and cafés and boutiques of country 'n' western gear. The music stores are, in fact, mostly pawn shops well supplied by musicians falling on hard times. Everywhere there are young Nashville cats guitar-picking at top speed. We looked at the rhinestone cowboy gear and I bought a couple more plastic jackets. The owner pressed us to bring the whole band along after the show but we escaped promising him a photo of the band for his wall - though no such photo was ever taken!

Back in '73 on the Ziggy tour with Fumble, David - the outrageous red-head - had received anonymous threats so that night the theatre was crawling with cops to protect him, a bizarre situation as many of them would have liked to carry out the threat themselves. As one said to Fumble, "We hate that fag Boo-wie but we love your rock 'n' roll!" So a couple of them came up to our dressing-room to chat and we tried on their caps and weighed their guns. One of them came round to the hotel the next day and drove us all round Nashville - his girlfriend even got us in to see the Grand Ole Oprey that night. He also took us to the store where they buy their uniforms and we were able to get a couple of genuine cop jackets - smart bomber-jackets with P for Police on the shiny silver buttons.

I tried to get in touch with an old friend called Mickey again, but in five years he had gone without trace.

After the show (which my diary reports as a bit subdued) we all went down to the hotel bar. It was dimly lit and David came in quietly among Tony, Frank and Coco. Soon after, a pretty crazy bunch of people filled the place. Matthew arrived with a few friends, strangely shy about being in the same bar as the Man. But they soon got busy mouthing off the crowd.

"Does Simon know that's a guy he's talking to? She's the most notorious drag queen in town." Matthew had to dissuade a girlfriend from tearing her wig off right there in the bar – I don't know why.

Coco came over and asked me if I knew a place to eat. Usually these discussions are carried on discretely, like spies, but this time David fancied somewhere lively so I asked my entourage. We ended up in a pretty noisy place with '30s decor and good food. It was pretty crowded and David caused a stir but he was able to eat in peace. He was at the next table to us with Dennis and a couple of sensational women and between the four of them they made more noise than anyone in the place.

★ ★ ★

In Memphis we stayed at a pleasant hotel built around two covered courtyards, one with a swimming-pool. After the show I jumped in the first taxi outside the hotel. The driver looked dour and his wife was sitting beside him with her knitting. I took a deep breath and asked, "Could you take me to a gay club please?" I went to a couple of quiet clubs and had a pleasant evening chatting to friendly people including a few who had seen the show.

Kansas City: an impressive airport with three huge circular terminals like space stations with planes nosing up to them. We drove in through a depressing industrial area to a luxurious modern hotel. The lobby featured a 'spectacular waterfall and indoor hillside garden' (according to the brochure).

Diary Notes:

Good gig though D a bit distracted first half.

After 'Rebel Rebel' we ran off-stage, piled into the limos and swung out of the car park before the 15,000 were moving. Back at the hotel there were other limousines unloading a party of revellers in tuxedos and long, expensive gowns. We stood about in our damp stage gear while Ron handed out our bags and bottles of booze from the gig. I then had to cross an acre of busy lobby in make-up, sweat and a silver plastic waistcoat (no shirt) with a large bag slung over one shoulder and a bottle of bourbon in my hand. I joined a smart group waiting for an elevator, then we all squeezed inside. I thought I was the only one who got out on my floor but as I sauntered down the corridor and fumbled with my room key I heard giggling and guessed I'd been followed.

"Hi, come in and have a drink," I suggested.

The two girls hesitated but followed me in when I came back with a bucket of ice. Linda and Jenny, brunette and blonde, a slinky black sheath and a white creation. I poured a couple of liberal Jack Daniels and coke, opened a cold beer for myself and tried to decide whether they were precocious fifteen or baby-doll twenty. I stuck some music on and disappeared into the shower. Five minutes later in jeans and T-shirt, I poured my first bourbon and heard how they had driven up from St. Louis to see the show. They told me what a dump St. Louis is, how they don't get on with their families but were soon off to college - Linda to dance in New York, Jenny to art college in LA.

The phone rang: "Hi!" It was Carlos smiling down the phone. "We're all meeting down in the bar to go to a club."

In the middle of the lobby was a sunken bar area overflowing with some of the 15,000. I introduced my protegés to Carlos and Simon and we were soon discussing the local night life over an expensive round of drinks. Kansas City spans two states. On one side of the river it's Kansas City, Kansas, where you can drink but it's dull. On the other side is Kansas City, Missouri, still dry from Prohibition but that's where all the clubs are - you can get a drink but it ain't easy, and a couple of phone calls put us off.

"How about a party here?" I suggested, sticking my neck out. I had visions of people throwing the TV out of the window, falling off the balcony, being sick all over the place, starting a fire and O/D-ing in the bathroom. Too late - everyone was heading for the elevators. The hotel management suddenly woke up (similar visions, no doubt) but too late - the lobby had cleared.

I filled a couple of trash cans with ice and beers and cokes – fortunately only one of them leaked – pushed the bed into a corner and stuck the TV in the closet. The cheap cassette player did its best and the place was soon pleasantly full without resembling a riot. I popped up to Pat and Eric's rooms, collecting more bottles and a small posse of fans lost in the corridors.

I can't remember whether David came or not – yes, it can get that way! Linda and Jenny kept going off then reappearing. A few people shut themselves in the bathroom with their dope – I don't know why they were so coy about it. I chatted here and there, relaxed but uninvolved. It was a civilised party – no headlines. Finally people started to drift off and then the room cleared quite swiftly. Usually at this point you're left with a few bodies, often stoned and some-times asleep, but now as the last couple departed I found myself alone with a girl I'd chatted to earlier. She was pretty but somehow not my type.

I stalled with another drink and we chatted some more. Inevitably there was soon a knock at the door and the 'Heavenly Twins' returned from one of their outings. They took a cool look and said "Goodnight". I was sorry to see them go.

My guest said she had a long way to drive home.

"Well, you're welcome to stay here – the bed's large and I won't attack you," I added, always the gentleman. When we were both in bed, I kissed her goodnight and she got more friendly but that didn't get us anywhere. So I kissed her goodnight again and turned over to go to sleep. I was just dozing off when the phone went. It was the 'twins': "I think I must have dropped my car keys in your room and we've got to leave."

I crawled out of bed stark naked to hunt for the damn things.

"They're not here," I told them, a few minutes later round the crack of the door.

My guest departed a few hours later. When I was woken at 10am, I was very glad to find a pineapple juice in one of the iced trash cans.

★ ★ ★

That afternoon we flew to Chicago - I remembered the airport from my arrival in America five weeks before: there were no direct flights from London to Dallas so I had to fly to Chicago and catch a connection. With two hours to change planes, there I planned a wash and shave and something to eat, but as we taxied in the tannoy asked "Would Mr. Mayes please identify himself to the cabin staff?" Two immigration officers escorted me from the plane. In their office I was told I had no proper visa - the travel agent had screwed up.

"We ought to fine you a thousand dollars and put you back on the next plane." They asked me how much money

I had and couldn't understand how someone could set out for the New World with only $20 cash and no credit cards. Somehow we all stayed polite and at last they let me through - "We're passing the buck to Dallas." I had just fifteen minutes to clear customs and get myself and my cases on to my connecting flight. In Dallas, immigration fined the airline $1000 for letting me fly without a visa! But today there were no problems of course.

We stayed at the Whitehall, a classic old hotel tucked in between the modern skyscrapers. Its decorated awning jutted confidently over the sidewalk and we were handed out by a liveried doorman. We were free that night and soon found the cost of all this elegance. Dinner would cost me a fortune and the restaurant was collar-and-tie. It's funny, after complaining about the faceless American hotels I had now got used to the convenience of a luxury cell-block.

Five minutes later I was out in a cold wind on the Chicago sidewalk. I soon found an ornate hamburger joint and ate an indifferent meal, watching the people, feeling content and thinking, *This is my first night in Chicago.*

When I got back, Carlos called me - he was in the bar with a friend, tall, blonde and even more elegant than the surroundings. Jane was studying singing, classical music and probably life. We went back to her apartment just around the corner - just around the corner and forty floors up. I gasped and grabbed the wall as we went in. The floor-to-ceiling window gaped on a bird's-eye view of Chicago by night.

The jagged music of *David Live* took over the room but she caught our pained expressions and replaced it with something more soothing – Chopin, I think.

We were there for a while drinking cognac and orange juice by turns, then went to a couple of clubs but nothing was happening. We ended the night at an all-night diner, one of those places with an ingrained atmosphere of exhausted sleeplessness.

The Auditorium Theatre is a 4000 seater and felt tiny after the stadiums. I was looking forward to this as I like to feel in touch with the whole audience. Unfortunately though, with the rig behind the proscenium arch and an orchestra pit beyond that we couldn't even see the front rows.

After the show Carlos, Coco and I found our way to a gay bar half a block away. It was pouring with rain and I carried Coco piggy-back as the streets were awash. The place was so full we had to fight our way to the bar. The guys on the door were friendly and wondered if David would be along later. I doubted it but didn't say so. The club-goers were decidedly cool though – we were a long way from the friendly south.

A few of our road crew appeared (the place was mixed) and I chatted to them. When I left, the guy on the door told me, "One of your people came in asking if he needed ID. I said, 'We don't need ID – just show us your meat!' And he brought it out – put it right there in my hand...!"

The following night at the theatre when the house lights went down, David asked for them to be turned back up a little, "so I can see you all out there." He got a cheer and the show went much better.

So simple-minded he can't drive his module
Bites on the neon and sleeps wherever he damn well pleases!

That night several of us went to a punk bar, La Mère Viper. It was a great place, a two-storey cellar painted black throughout with aerosol graffiti everywhere. There were bizarre decorations such as shreds of white paper hanging from the ceiling where neon lighting zig-zagged crazily above the dancers. It was refreshing after all the plastic hotels and clubs. We were made very welcome and couldn't pay for a drink. The music was loud and fast and we joined the jumping crowd under the neon lights.

I climbed the rickety stairs to the men's room. I was splashing water on my hair to make it more spiky when a guy staggered in, very drunk. He started to mutter something to me about Bowie and the show but with no sign of recognising me. Then he focussed on me and the truth struck him – literally! He fell back against the wall and slid down it. Then he struggled up and grabbed my hand. "It's you? You're from the show...! Must have an autograph... sign... sign my arm... no pen..." Suddenly he tore open his shirt – "Scratch me!" he said urgently. I found an eyebrow-pencil, autographed his arm and left him there propped against the wall, admiring the souvenir.

Back at the hotel, Dennis was throwing a loud and happy party. David was cheerful though a few people were quizzing him about his work. I met a guy who turned out to be a mild S&M fan – quite fun in the heat of the moment but uncomfortable for the next couple of days... He still writes though...

CHAPTER 6

THE LAKES

Wednesday, 19th April

In Detroit we stayed in a smart hotel right on the river – so smart I had to wait for my luggage and squeeze into my white stage jeans before they'd let me in the restaurant. None of us went out that night – we were warned about the streets in that area and decided to wait for daylight before risking our health.

From my high window I could look down on Cobo Hall, the large round building where we were playing tomorrow. I also had a good view of the river and an enormous suspension bridge linking Michigan and Canada.

Next day I went for a windy walk to the Renaissance Centre, a cluster of silver cylinders housing a multi-level shopping centre, all hanging plants and running water –

bright boutiques in a concrete jungle. I found a toy shop with plastic creatures swimming about in a tank so I bought a dolphin to give David as a joke, but later this seemed too whimsical and it sank to the bottom of my suitcase along with other souvenirs.

I had a solitary sandwich in the café there and the waitress asked if I was with DB. She was rather sweet and I put her on the guest list for a couple of tickets. Next day a basket of roses arrived with a note of thanks which touched me – thank you!

Cobo Hall was a great place to play – 12,000 is a good size and the crowd were wild, really jumping. Rough cities usually have great audiences – Glasgow, Hamburg, Detroit – they either love you or hate you and really let you know it. In the second half, kids were coming down the front, taking photos, throwing scarves, waving banners, photos, anything to attract his attention. But what soon attracted mine was the violence of the bouncers who were really laying into the kids. That kind of thing makes it hard to play, and as one of the group there's nothing you can do – except wait for David to notice. I caught Carlos' eye. We were playing 'Ziggy Stardust' and we could feel David was unhappy. He fluffed a couple of lines then waved his arms – "Stop! Stop that! You – and you... we don't need you! Get out!" The husky voice rang out in the hall and the crowd stirred.

The men looked up, sullen and embarrassed in the loud silence, the lights on them. Eric was down at the front in a flash, grabbing them, hustling them out – he's come close to being beaten up himself a few times confronting bouncers.

The music started again but David blew the next line, too upset to sing. So Carlos started the grinding guitar phrase of 'Suffragette City' and as we all swung into the pounding intro, the crowd cheered and David used his adrenalin to spit out the lines... *Hey man! Ah, leave me alone, you know! Hey man!* The crowd shouted and stomped along and the mood was broken.

Up in my room, I pulled a cold beer from my stage bag and stripped off my wet clothes. Down below, the crowds streamed out of the hall and a couple of fire engines and cop cars screamed up to the entrance, lights flashing. I don't know what the trouble was but they didn't stay long.

Down in the lobby, Carlos grabbed me – "Hey punk, come and meet these girls!" Patti, Diane and two Kims had come from Toronto in Canada for the gig and squeezed into the cheapest room in the hotel. We went out to a couple of dull places then back to the hotel with two giant pizzas and took them up to my room. The pizzas were so large we only ate one between us. The next day I tossed the other one on top of the closet to get it out of the way. Unfortunately the closet had no top so the two-foot pizza 'with everything' cascaded down all over my clothes, coming to rest on a pair of boots.

That night we did another exciting show, this time with no trouble, then Carlos and I met up with the girls and went to a bar with original '30s decor just like classic Hollywood. Sitting around the place like extras from a sci-fi film were Detroit's punks in all their spiky splendour.

* * *

We left Detroit for Cleveland, Ohio. The city looked dreary and dirty as we flew in over Lake Erie. We drove to Swingo's Inn, a rock 'n' roll hotel, a favourite with musicians. As we got out of the cars, I saw Dennis shaking hands with a stocky, elderly black man in a navy blue cap. I thought he was one of the chauffeurs but it was actually Count Basie who was playing in town with Ella Fitzgerald. Dennis knows the Count and Tony Mascia used to drive for him in New York. Unfortunately their show was at the same time as ours.

It was good to be staying in a place with a bit of character. The wallpaper was very dark and there was a shabby black leather sofa. The raffia blind was drawn against the bright afternoon sun and the place had a shadowy, Eastern air.

I got a call from the desk asking if I knew a Miss so-and-so (Patti and Co.) as they wanted to stay in a room next to mine. I said, "Fine," not realising David was also nearby. Here I was screwing up security again!

We were all called in for a meeting with David, Pat and Eric about the next album. I was really excited - I never imagined I would end up on a Bowie album.

I took a stroll along Mainstreet – small, quiet and mostly closed as it was a Saturday afternoon. I bought a film for my camera and another pair of striped socks.

The stadium was quite a place – 30,000 – and the dressing-room was large and comfortable. I had run out of gel so I poured beer on my hair – it was ideal as it dried nice and spiky but washed off easily and probably did it good!

We had a police escort out into the hall as we had to pass through public areas. The cops had the usual dead-pan expressions which they wear around rock musicians and I got the usual tingle down my back that I get around cops. The show started quietly but built steadily as if the vast crowd was gathering momentum until the show was a landslide.

If you think we're gonna make it
You better hang on to yourse-e-elf…

Later I met up with Carlos and a couple of the girls. We went to the Agora Club where Iggy had played with David on piano – Patti gave me some photos showing David looking elegantly downbeat behind a small upright. I thought the club might be fun but it was very quiet – maybe everyone went to our show! I went out and called a cab. The driver sourly informed me that there were no gay bars in Cleveland. I didn't argue but had him take me back to the hotel.

The bar was now full and the cabaret group seemed uncomfortably aware of a presence. I joined Patti and her friends and we ended up at a table next to David and Co. We nodded to each other but Patti was struck dumb – terrified.

"Do you want to say hello to him? I'll introduce you."

She shook her head and shrank further into her seat and her misery. I felt amused and exasperated by turns. What a night! Finally we got up to leave at the same time and all ended up crowded together in the elevator, getting out on the same floor, saying "Goodnight."

I got back to my room and closed the door, leaning against it with a sigh. There was a knock. Oh God. I opened it, frowning. It was a girl I'd never seen before.

"Hello, I, er... I saw you in the corridor..." She seemed very shy and embarrassed – almost surprised to find herself doing this.

"Come in and have a drink," I said, feeling nothing, suspended between moods. She was pleasant-looking but not dressed like she was out for the night. I poured her a bourbon and coke, opened a beer for myself.

"I saw you in the bar – I wanted someone to talk to." She spoke with the intensity of a student explaining a theory. "You looked... you looked like you might be sympathetic."

"Did you see the show?" – for something to say.

"What show?"

I told her. Well, there's no reason why someone shouldn't drop into a hotel bar without realising who had just hit town. Probably fifty per cent of the people in Cleveland didn't know or care about Mr. B. It just never feels like that when you're part of the circus.

"I suppose that's why the bar was so crowded," she said.

I don't think we even exchanged names for a long time, but we began to talk and the circus faded. She had been brought up in a convent, now she was married but it wasn't going right. She felt trapped by her surroundings. We talked for several hours and she left as the sky was lightening.

I was late down to breakfast and just ordered coffee. Todd Rundgren was passing through – Roger played in Todd's band but was having time off like me. He introduced me to Todd and his friends. I'm not good at meeting people first thing in the day and couldn't think of a thing to say – I had never heard his music. So I just asked politely if they had finished their breakfast then helped myself before Eric came to chase us into the cars. Sorry Todd.

So we flew to Milwaukee. I should think we made a fairly distinctive group at airports, not like the average businessmen who fill the planes. Dennis is never without his 30 inch circular cymbal bag decorated with appliqué leather Red Indian designs. He carried anything but cymbals in it. I probably looked the most unlikely one in short, tight, rolled-up jeans and hung-about with bulging shoulder-bag, cassette player (this was pre-Walkman days), camera, typewriter and an old briefcase full of cassettes. I was usually rushing about the place looking for food or postcards or a paper with last night's review. David was a more elegant figure, a water-colour sketch of soft hues – short hair with the translucence of the natural near-blond, his face a gentle tan, long trench-style raincoat in the palest olive, light JAL shoulder bag. This quiet figure was the unconscious centre of the maelstrom.

★ ★ ★

Milwaukee. We were not playing that night so I decided to ease up on the late-night lifestyle and dined on partridge with Pat and Eric in the hotel's elegant restaurant. The elegance unfortunately stopped short at the decor and the bird was tough and tasteless. I had one glass of wine then saw a movie with some of the band and went to bed thinking how healthy and rested I should feel in the morning.

It was 7am when the stomach pains hit me and I crawled into the bathroom for the first explosion of diarrhoea. Cursing last night's partridge, I took something to settle my stomach and buried myself in bed again. Later Carlos rang to say he'd arranged an interview with a local paper and could they all come up to my room. I got up and dressed and decided I would survive. Adrian and Simon arrived with the reporters, three guys and a girl with a camera, a small cassette recorder and a couple of back-copies of their music paper. One of the guys told us his wife was having a baby in a hospital outside Milwaukee "but I had to come to town as David was here." I think this event may have spoiled his concentration. They had no idea what questions to ask so we just talked about the tour and told them things we thought they'd like to know.

We went over for a sound-check. The hall had strange acoustics and we remixed the piano. The dressing-rooms were comfortable and I relaxed on one of the sofas with a brandy and water. The show went really well and I was carried along on the tide of it with no great effort. Few big tours ever come to Milwaukee, so the crowd really had a ball. Some of them looked appealing and the hall was close to the hotel but there was no way I could make it. I showered and went straight to bed.

Next morning I still felt bad but struggled down for a late, light breakfast with Frank and a couple of girls. One of them told us she had driven down from up-state and certainly lost her job by coming. "I've probably lost my husband too," she added ruefully.

It was a long flight to Pittsburgh. I nibbled a little of the meal then later turned white, then green and nearly passed out. There was a pharmacy at the hotel so I took their best stuff and went straight to bed. The phone was on the other side of the room and that night I got several calls from kids who just hung up.

Next morning I was too weak to stand. I crawled to the phone and asked for a doctor. The hotel telephonist sounded like a friendly mum and I felt really pathetic and far from home. The floor manager came up and I was taken out to a cab in a wheelchair. At the hospital I had various unpleasant tests then the doctor told me I'd picked up a bug from drinking tap water - even 'safe' water can make you ill if you're from a different continent. It couldn't be food poisoning - it wasn't bad enough! It made Milwaukee very memorable... next time I'll stick to beer. Promising the doctor a couple of tickets, I returned to the hotel and bed with a bottle of pills. Everyone phoned to see how I was and 'Mum' would always ask too, which was nice.

That night I was excused the sound-check. A limo took me to the hall just before we went on. Somehow I rallied and coped with the show, feeling quite a hero.

CHAPTER 7

THE EAST COAST AND CANADA

Thursday, 27th April

Washington - a beautiful city, European in flavour like many on the east coast. We strolled in from the airport down broad tree-lined avenues, past the slim white stone pencil of the Washington Monument, 500 feet high. The cars swept up to the Watergate Hotel, much smarter than our usual haunts, part of the famous Watergate complex where Nixon's problems began. We cracked a few jokes about bugging. I bought a copy of *All The President's Men* at a book-stall, partly as a souvenir.

By now I was rather blasé about the places we stayed but I wasn't prepared for the palatial suite which awaited me at the Watergate - an open-plan apartment with vast bed, complete dining suite and a couple of large sofas. Long curtains swung gently in the breeze and French windows opened onto a large balcony overlooking the Potomac River and a sweep of the countryside. It was good to have left behind the flat starkness of the Mid-Western cities.

I got down to the lobby early and found the limos waiting. I nearly went and got in but suddenly a grim party in dark suits marched through the lobby and into the cars, in their midst the familiar eye-patch of Moshe Dayan, Israel's military leader until 1974. I hate to think of those armed guards finding me reclining in their limousine! It was a long drive to the gig and there were road signs up saying 'DAVID BOWIE'.

That night, after the gig, I strolled down to the lobby feeling that my gorgeous suite was demanding a party though I hardly felt up to it. The dignified lobby was not teeming with fans, just two women, black and sensational.

"Hi, is David coming down?"

"I don't know, I haven't heard from him."

"Do you know where we can call him - we know him, you see."

My heart sank. Everybody "knows David" but I couldn't see myself putting these two off easily. We went to the Spanish Bar, quiet, almost empty. One of them was walking with a stick but I made no comment.

"I'm Sandie," she said, "and this is my cousin Martie. I did back-up vocals on one of David's tours."

We chatted over expensive drinks then David arrived

with Coco and Frank and embraced the girls, delighted to
see them.

"What have you done to your leg?" he asked Sandie.

"Oh, someone beat me up," she said with a wry smile.

David told us how he had come close to a brush with
Moshe Dayan earlier on.

"On the way in from the airport we passed three long
black cars and one of them came out and buzzed us – didn't
seem to like being overtaken. Then I think they worried
when we took the same highway turn-off but Tony left
them behind."

We laughed at the thought of them checking up on
David's car at the hotel.

The bar chairs all had castor wheels so when the bar
finally closed David and I pushed Sandie along the corridor
to the stairs and Frank carried her up to the lobby.

I returned the chair to the bar by which time everyone
had vanished. I soon fell asleep in palatial splendour, only to
be up and packing again the next morning.

★ ★ ★

Friday – Philadelphia! This was the first place we played in
the States back in 1973.

I've still got a photo of the Tower Theatre hoarding:

'FEB 16-19th DAVID BOWIE AND THE SPIDERS
FROM MARS – FUMBLE.'

It was bitterly cold that February, the snow gusting about grittily like sand. Driving into the theatre in a long airport taxi, the driver asked what we were doing. "We're playing with David Bowie." A grunt - Bowie in '73 was the last word in decadence. Then Barry, our drummer, who only smoked Gauloises or Gitanes, asked innocently, "Is there anywhere here we can get French fags?"

"Kinda choosy, ain't ya?" muttered the cabbie nastily.

That time we did seven shows in four days to the then-staggering total of 20,000 people. The word 'fumble' turned out to be an American football expression so it really caught on and even the cops outside used to shout it when they saw us arrive - and David himself took up the shout one night on-stage.

Of course, things were different this time.

We were staying at the Hilton Inn next to the gig, the 15,000 seater Spectrum. I missed being in town but there was still a great feeling of being back somewhere familiar. This had been the first American city to make David a star. Now we were back to make his second live album (*Stage*) here.

We went across early for a special sound-check. Tony Visconti was there in the recording truck parked in the vast back-stage area. The sound was taken unmixed straight from the rig, plus a mike suspended high in the auditorium for ambience.

David doesn't like too much crowd noise on a live album - he feels it's in bad taste but I miss this on *Stage* as it seems part of the show. I've always been a sucker for live gigs and crowd reaction.

I didn't miss any that night in Philadelphia. The atmosphere as we came on-stage was electric and joyous. Usually there's a smattering of crazy costumes but tonight it was a bright-eyed fancy dress parade which soon became a Roman carnival.

The stage light blazed back at us off make-up and tinsel - jagged lightning and white mime faces, henna and bleach jobs plus some of the classiest most sensational of sexy chic evening wear - slashed skirts and dark stockings, fur and feathers, leather and skin - and more skin as bikini tops were abandoned to the dance. There was an air of sensual arousal and some of the smiles that turned up to David were as glittering as his own.

My mind was split between the effort of concentrating - trying not to take my usual handfuls of notes, imagining poor Tony thinking, *How are we going to hide that?* But I soon abandoned myself to the fun, the crowd squealing with delight from the slow gong beats of 'Warsawa' to the disco bump and grind of 'Fame'. Dave Fudger did an excellent review of this gig in *Sounds*. It's a strange feeling for me to drop into the crowd with him for a moment:

"After eleven songs he speaks to the audience: 'Hello.' Pause for cheers.

'We'll be seeing you again in ten minutes. Will you be here?' (Of course they will be!) 'Thank you for coming.'

Then he's off with the band and the lights come up. Through the smoke haze it's just possible to read the illuminated TASTYKAKE ad on the opposite side of the hall. To recorded intermission music by the Rutles, Iggy and Lou Reed (Bowie's choice) the kids play with frisbees, beach balls and giant balloons, or consume hideous hamburgers, milk-shakes, soft drinks, popcorn, ice-cream and more grass."

The second half with Ziggy was predictably an explosion. Here in Philadelphia, I had seen Ziggy in '73. That first night I had been astonished to see the Man, just about to go on, in a black leather Japanese-style outfit with legs so wide and stiff, like wings, he could hardly walk. That's silly, David, I thought. But he waddled onto the strobe-lit stage, the flame of his red hair the only colour in that silver flicker, Beethoven's 'Song Of Joy' gave way to 'Hang On' then he stood, arms outstretched, while two girls in black ran on and tore the suit off him. ("It's held together with poppers but I nearly fell over some nights when they didn't pull together!") He emerged like a butterfly from a cocoon in a blaze of white silk... *Ziggy played guitar...*

This time, his white trousers are scarcely less baggy than those black leather but he has no trouble moving. It was a joyful romp and he even did the space-face specs to a roar of delight. *Aaaah - Wham Bam Thank You Ma'am* must have bent the needles in the recording truck.

Finally – *It's not the side effect of the cocaine, I'm thinking that it must be love!* All the lights blazing forth on the orgy before us, we bounced back for the encore then leapt for the limos as if the crowd were at our heels for the short dash back to the hotel. There from my window I could see The Spectrum rising like the Rome Coliseum from acres of arc-lit cars as the black ant-like crowd streamed out, heading for the night's traffic jam or the subway... or, of course, the hotel.

Feeling healthier than I had for a few days, I was soon dropping down to the lobby. As the elevator doors slid back I was plunged into a scene of frantic confusion. The place was so full of surging kids I had difficulty in getting out while a (literally) hard-pressed security guy tried to stop them getting in. I was grabbed, squealed at, asked for autographs, had my hands shaken and was continually asked, "When is David coming down?" I slowly pushed my way through, searching. Then I caught sight of the spiky hair and disentangled myself from the eager bunch of kids around me. Here were three punks from the front row, as sweet and nasty as I remembered. We gazed at each other for a charged moment which seemed to suspend the noise around us.

"Hi, boys, where's the best gay bar in town?"

We went to a couple of places. One was pleasantly scruffy like a British coffee bar in the '60s. We ended up in a large club, a smart disco where I did my DB band member bit to get us in.

Clyde was a thin, angular youth with short spiky hair and impossible (but real!) eyelashes. He had an unerring eye for the bizarre and outrageous, his clothes a wild mixture of

New York punk boutique and Philly thrift stores. Paul was his flat mate, John a friend. Clyde and I chatted in a corner while the music raged about our heads.

Later we grabbed a cab back to the hotel.

Things were quieter now, though the all-night coffee shop was overflowing. Philadelphia certainly makes an event of it when David comes to town. Some of the kids were still there next morning but that was nothing to their endurance. Back in February, scores of them had camped in the snow for tickets on the windswept Spectrum parking lot. Before someone froze to death, Clyde made a list of the people and got the box office to agree to it.

Next morning, it took bravado to enter that coffee shop feeling every eye was on us. We found a table. I signed one or two autographs and a couple of Clyde's friends came over for a word. I noticed some of the road crew, wondering if they were surprised. As one of the band I would never be shown a reaction by these Texan cowboys of course.

Fortified with breakfast, we went into town, made coffee at Clyde's place and woke Paul. It was Saturday and felt like a holiday, a break from touring. We went out – it was a lovely area, tree-lined streets, old rose brick houses, almost a village feeling.

Friends of theirs said "Hi!" and I felt I wasn't in a strange town.

We had a long rehearsal that afternoon – last night's tape showed that everything was going too fast, so Carlos re-established the studio tempos. I felt this was too slow. It's natural for numbers to go a little faster live, as long as they don't run away with it. Later on, I think we achieved the best feeling – a shade faster than the records, exciting but controlled.

Tonight, Clyde and his friends only managed the second row. It was good but strange to see them there, breaking the usual anonymity of the crowd. A public performance is a very private thing – like performing in front of a mirror!

The show felt strange with Carlos holding down the speed of numbers but it was still another crazy, happy night from the first boom of 'Warsawa' to the last bounce of 'Rebel Rebel'. Then we rushed to the cars for the quick spin to the hotel, from the lights of The Spectrum parking lot to the lights of the Hilton parking lot. Kids who hadn't been able to get tickets were already crowded around the entrance for a glimpse and a skirmish as David, a blue dressing-gown and the massive arm of Tony around his shoulders, swept through the lobby to be beamed up in the elevator. The rest of us followed with less style.

I collected Clyde and a few friends and we went up to my room under the watchful eye of the floor managers, one posted outside the elevator and another at the fire-exit. I hadn't realised before but David's suite was right opposite my room. We sat around drinking and chatting and someone rolled a joint. They thumbed through my photos from the early part of the tour and we talked about the tour, the show, New York, Philadelphia, people – "Did you see Purple and her friend swinging their tits in the third row?!"

Next day, Sunday, Clyde and I got down to breakfast about 1pm – omelettes and coffee. There weren't so many kids around today. We wandered out to the bright but windy parking lot. A youth came up to us and insisted that Clyde was Bowie, just for something to say, maybe. There are some strange people in the world and you are sure to encounter a few on a Bowie tour!

We went back in and I finished packing.

We were off to Canada and it was time to say "Goodbye". "I'll try to hitch up to New York when you're there." We remembered to kiss before leaving the room – outside it was just a quick hug then I climbed into a limo leaving Clyde to get a cab back into town. I felt dazed and a bit down. I was going to miss him.

We were flying to Toronto. I should have been excited, I'd never been to Canada before. We had been warned about Customs – not to carry anything through as we were bound to be searched. In the event, we were treated as VIPs and David signed a couple of autographs for the officers!

Next morning I felt much brighter. The sun was shining and here I was in Canada.

Patti and Kim came round (we met in Detroit) and took me to a hairdresser where I was soon the centre of attention.

Everyone discussed the colour and what he should use,

how long it should be left on and "I wonder if David needs a haircut?"

Maple Leaf Gardens is the stadium of a famous team. Many of the road crew were sporting Maple Leaf T-shirts but I never managed to get one. There were some new tour shirts being handed out though - smart ones in black and orange with David as the Gigolo.

We rehearsed 'Alabama Song' which replaced 'Rock 'n' Roll Suicide' and became a compulsive hit of the tour.

When we got back after the show, I got a call from David to say he was with Lindsay Kemp in the bar. I found them right at the back in the gloom with a couple of Lindsay's mime troupe - Jack, known as the Great Orlando, and a beautiful young man called David. Lindsay was doing a season in Toronto with *Salomé* and *Flowers* and the three of them had been to see the show.

Lindsay and Jack both had shaven heads.

Lindsay was shrugged into a vast and colourful jacket of Tudor proportions while Jack was dressed simply and strikingly in black. He played Borgia Ginz in *Jubilee*.

Everyone seemed tired and conversation was sporadic - I made no notes of any gems!

Next day we flew to Ottawa. I don't remember too much about the place. We played the Civic Centre which reminded me of a large gym, though it held 10,000 people.

Some cities excite me when I first arrive in them, often for no apparent reason.

Montreal just had an air about it and I felt suddenly fresh and alert. Perhaps it was the contrasts - old and new, French and English. Our hotel, Le Régence Hyatt, was very modern but with more style than most.

I was hoping to trace a friend of mine from a few years back in Switzerland. I had an address but no phone number so set off in a cab with Kim who had come over by train from Toronto. It was a long street of dilapidated houses. I knocked at the door and after a long wait a bearded face appeared, half asleep. He didn't seem to understand what I was saying and was shutting the door when I came out with some French. The change was immediate!

He opened the door and was now delighted to see us: "Ah, you are Michel's friend, yes, I haven't seen him for a couple of days, he lives with his girlfriend most of the time now."

Leo, wrapped in a dressing-gown, led us through to the scruffy kitchen and soon we were sipping instant coffee from chipped mugs. I really enjoyed all this, getting away from the eternal deluxe. We made plans for the evening - Leo would get in touch with Michel.

At the Montreal Forum there was a bit of a bomb scare - nothing too serious - apparently, there is always a bomb scare. They had to check the area under the stage in case a French (Quebec) Nationalist had planted something. The show went very well but David didn't sing "Heroes" in French though the single was out in both languages here.

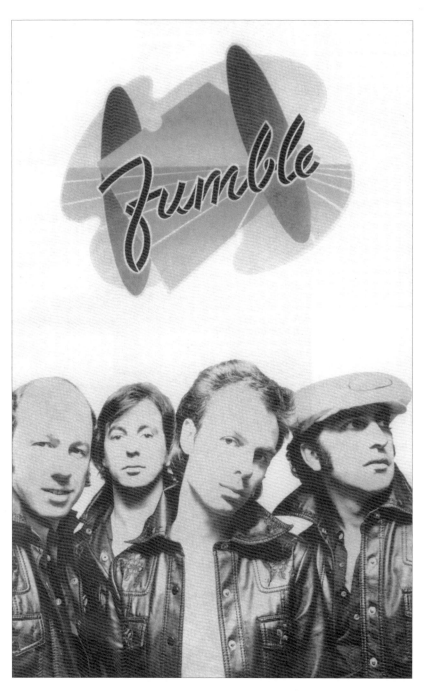

Fumble: Barry Pike, Des Henley, Sean Mayes and Mario Ferrari

Left: Sean in rehearsal.

Right: Iggy Pop in Edinburgh.

Left: Rehearsals in Australia.

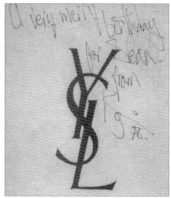

Above: David and friends relaxing in Perth.

Below left: David photographs the audience in Auckland, New Zealand.

Above: Fast food in Harlem.

Below left: The Bodyguards: Stuey
George (left) and the late Tony Mascia
in Australia.

Right: Sean at work on the diary.

Above: Left to right: Roger Powell, George Murray, Carlos Alomar, Adrian Belew, (a roadie) and David at the LA Forum.

Below left: on stage in the UK and *below right* in rehearsal.

Left: David and Brian Eno at work in Switzerland, 1978.

Below: Tony Visconti, David and Brian Eno recording *Lodger* at Mountain Studio, Switzerland.

Above: Carlos Alomar at home in New York.

Below: Sean, Dennis Davis, Simon House and George Murray.

ISOLAR II

BOWIE 78

GUEST PASS

Above: Sean and friends at the end of tour *Gigolo* party in Japan.

Below: David's signature in Japanese.

In honor of David Bowie you are cordially invited to a 'gigolo party' on December 12, 1978 at 10:30pm at Bee, Roppongi.

Dress: 1920's style optional black tie

R.S.V.P. (03)499-3621 Miss Holke

"I can't remember the words now," he said when I asked him.

After the show I met Leo and Michel and we went to a French restaurant with a few friends. It was packed, noisy and cheerful, we spoke French all night and it was hard to believe I was still on the North American continent.

Next morning I had a badly needed orange juice then went down to the lobby to grab some postcards and food. I was sorry to be leaving Montreal but excited to be going to Boston and the last leg of the American tour.

CHAPTER 8

BOSTON AND NEW YORK

Thursday, 4th May

We touched down in Boston on American soil again, late in the afternoon and drove to The Sheraton where I soon felt at home. My room was large and comfortable and as we were there for three nights, I unpacked all my books and put up a few cards and my Elvis poster. Coco called me – his lordship was staying in to watch TV and maybe doze, so we went out to a Chinese restaurant with some of the band.

I ordered a fish dish which turned out to be the whole thing, two feet of it! Then Coco and I rushed off to see a film. When we returned to The Sheraton, Clyde was there in the lobby, looking as out of place as... well, a punk in a hotel lobby! I restrained myself from rushing up and hugging him and the three of us went up to my room. Between us we had enough nickels and dimes for a couple of cans of coke from the machine down the corridor. I opened a bottle of bourbon and we sat around like students discussing Americans and Europeans, sex and philosophy till the small hours.

Next day, Clyde and I went out to the shops. I didn't see anything special but in a men's store we were surprised to meet Steve, an old school friend of Clyde's. He was due for his lunch break so we went and had breakfast in an old Boston tea room then Clyde and I caught the subway back, a sort of underground tram complete with overhead powerlines.

The gig that night was in Providence, about an hour's drive away. I dozed most of the way, ate too much before the show and didn't really enjoy it. This gig was also recorded for the live album. Clyde had stayed behind to meet Steve and when I got back my room was dim and full of smoke and music. They were propped up on the floor with a joint, a large bottle of wine at hand. I swigged some while I changed then we went out to a couple of gay bars – typical American places, very butch and spit 'n' sawdust. I couldn't imagine any of them going to a Bowie concert. Still, it seemed to fit my mood and I was able to unwind and relax.

Next day we had a late breakfast of Eggs Benedict – we seemed to be living on the coffee-shop menu. Then I got down to writing scores of postcards. Everyone back home wants a card from the States.

The limos took us to the Boston Garden, home of the Boston Bruins. While Dennis was pounding his drums for the sound-check I slipped away to the pro sports shop, a glorious place full of T-shirts, sweat-shirts, hats, caps and jackets as well as the regular sports gear and all so cheap. I stocked up on '50s gear for Fumble then rushed back to have Eric shout at me for being late.

It was a great gig but with one drawback – the 'Boston rock-thrower'. The last few times Dennis had played the place – with David and with George Benson – someone had thrown stones at the stage. At first I thought this was one of Dennis' funny stories but that night two huge rocks were thrown, one narrowly missing Dennis, the other smashing one of Roger's keyboards. What a crazy situation! At nearly every gig in Boston, this character picks up a couple of rocks from the car park then at some point in the show stands up – "Excuse me!" – and lobs the rocks onto the stage.

Clyde got back to the hotel soon after me.

Steve had gone to a Witch Sabbath do. We had a snack and headed out to The Rat, Boston's new-wave club (*Let's go to The Rat, oh baby…*). People crowded round to congratulate me on the show and we were soon grabbed by a girl called Ricci. She had wild blonde hair, black tights on her long legs and wore a very sharp spiked bracelet which seemed to be more than just decorative. She adopted the two of us on the spot and when The Rat closed, Ricci and her friend took us back to their apartment, a large place, sparsely furnished. We sat around and drank and a joint passed to the strains of 'Love You Till Tuesday'. Then Ricci showed me her room with a water-bed, a synth and a bass guitar. We made some loud free-form noise then I bounced on the bed to see what it felt like.

Walking back later, Clyde commented, "I wondered if you two were making it."

"Mmm, it did cross my mind but neither of us made a move so here I am!"

Next day we were off to New York, so I got permission to catch a train there with Clyde and had the most enjoyable trip of the tour. While the others piled into the limos for the half-hour drive to the airport, Clyde and I fell into a beat-up old cab for a five-minute scoot to the rail station. There we caught a silver monster which gently rocked us through three states of countryside and coastline in the sort of sunshine we usually only see above the clouds.

Four hours later, Clyde explained the layout of Manhattan Island while the train wound its way through the tenements. It's a slim island, thirteen miles by two-and-a-half.

Most of the streets are deep canyons between high buildings where shafts of sunlight slope down, only touching the road for a brief moment of each day. We emerged from Grand Central, bags in hand, walked a few blocks to admire the art deco facing of the Empire State Building then hailed a yellow cab and headed uptown to the Westbury.

This was an elegant old-style hotel on Madison Avenue,

one block from Central Park. We entered the elegant but gloomy lobby and I collected my key. If the elderly porters thought us strange they gave no sign. We creaked slowly up in the elevator with its silent operator. The furniture was ornate - high brass beds and stiff upright armchairs, brocade curtains with elaborate pelmets - well, it made a change!

Carlos was throwing a birthday party that night in Hurrah's, one of the top discos. We arrived much too early and wandered about eyeing the food. A good-looking crowd of all colours soon flooded in. Slim beautiful people dressed to kill. Or at least to maim.

One gorgeous black girl with very short hair was wearing a second skin of brilliant white sharkskin which looked as if God had made it to measure. Jimmy, Carlos' cousin, had made an elaborate cake which was a big success. People started to dance, the pace hotted up. Clyde knew a few people and we chatted to the boss who invited us to a '60s new-wave party the following night.

David put in a brief appearance. "Your boss really is quite a fox," observed Clyde dryly. The fox disappeared into the crowd of bodies on the dance floor and I didn't see him again. Coco joined us later when he had gone. "He was rather shy about coming here tonight as several of his ex-girlfriends were here. But you should have seen their faces when he walked in." David had walked in with Bianca - his first public appearance with Mrs. Jagger. And we missed it!

Next morning we were soon on the subway heading downtown to the Village.

There are plenty of little cafés doing all sorts of breakfasts and snacks. We wandered around, passing the wedge-shaped building that used to be a women's prison where they would lean out of the windows and shout good-natured abuse and Clyde and his friends would shout back.

The Village had a nice feel after the glass 'n' concrete canyons uptown. The streets cross at all angles and the buildings are older and lower, shabby and interesting.

You can cross the street when you want to, the automobile doesn't rule.

We ran into Jim, Judy and Cathy from Philly - rather a remote coincidence in a way but it seemed natural in the friendly atmosphere of the Village. They gave me a lift back to the hotel where I grabbed my things and the limos were soon nosing their way through the rush hour traffic, downtown to West 31st and Madison Square Garden. One minute we were shouldering our way between the yellow cabs on a six-lane street then the next we swung into the gloom of the great round building, purring up the circular ramp which spirals up five levels.

The impression of being in a Roman amphitheatre was immediate and for one overwhelming reason: as we opened the doors of the air-conditioned cars we were hit by the pungent smell of animals - it had to be... elephants? It was elephants - and lions, tigers, camels...Yes, it was the Barnum

& Bailey Circus! They do a month's residency at Madison Square Garden and Pat had to buy them out for two nights - but out didn't mean right out. The complete menagerie was just along the passage on our level.

They even brought the elephants out among the limousines to water them - the imperial transport of two ages and two continents side by side.

I walked through into the vast volume of the stadium. It was breathtakingly large, but in a funny way I was disappointed. I had expected some kind of concert hall, not another sports stadium. There is something about a theatre that I find more exciting than any stadium, however big. Still, this was New York, this was the Garden, and I was excited.

Back in the dressing-rooms, Adrian was terrified. "Bob Fripp will be out there... Earl Slick may be coming..." Everyone was uneasy at the reputation of the place and the people coming but in my innocence I felt very relaxed. I didn't know what piano players might be out front so I wasn't going to start worrying. I just thought, *This is New York and I'm going to have a ball!*

And I did - right through the first set till somewhere in 'Beauty and the Beast' when I looked round and saw Bianca and Coco standing about twelve feet behind me...

That shook me more than any musician I could think of and I finished the set unsteadily.

WHAT'S YOUR NAME? whatsyourname whatsyour-name?ame?

When we came off and were running for the limos, I passed Bianca and grinned at her in the euphoria of the moment. She gave a small smile.

I hadn't been in long when Patti and Kim from Toronto arrived hotfoot from the Greyhound station having scraped their last dollars together to be in at the end. Clyde soon joined us and we all headed for Hurrah's again for the '60s new-wave party.

This was fun but not a huge success as people didn't dance much with no disco music. There were a few familiar faces from the front of the gig including one girl I'd noticed in a cut-away lace-up T-shirt. She made one-off clothes and was looking for buyers. She and Clyde suggested going to Studio 54.

"Studio 54?" I queried.

"Haven't you heard of it? It's the top disco in New York - Barbra Streisand, Mick Jagger and people go there."

"Don't you have to be members?"

"No, you all stand outside and the doorman looks at everyone and lets you in if he likes the look of you."

"Sounds crazy!"

It was only a short cab ride to 54th Street.

There was a small area off the sidewalk and people were standing around pressing against the plush velvet rope. There were a couple of young guys inside the magic circle and one of them peered over the heads and spotted us, then waved people aside as he parted the rope. We sailed in, trying not to grin, and even sauntered on past the desk without paying.

This was the first hi-tech disco I had seen, a large converted cinema well-stocked with beautiful people. Space-age lighting descended among the dancers and topless waiters cutely attired in white silk boxer-shorts brought drinks to the tables. At the bar everyone looked fashionably bored while the barman danced a disco jig, tossing the cocktail shaker.

We watched the dancers for a while then wandered up through the maze of rooms above finding a corner where the beat was only a pulse and chatted till three.

Next day we met Linda in the Village and wandered around till it was time for me to head back for the last gig of the US tour.

This time we didn't see the elephants but a monkey on roller skates came to visit us in the dressing-rooms. Far less disconcerting was Brian Eno, a lovely man, who came in and chatted diffidently. I took a photo of him with Roger while they eagerly discussed the different ways in which Brian had created the sounds on *Low* and *"Heroes"* and Roger recreated them on-stage.

We played an exuberant bitter-sweet gig, blowing farewell to America *YOU...*

YOU CAN BE ME... 20,000 rocked Madison Square... *WE CAN BE HEROES!*

Tonight we had the run of the limos, extra large ones with

a fridge and TV, so we joined some of the band and their wives and floated down to CBGB's in extravagant style. But this joint was not jumping, so we headed back to Studio 54 where I met a couple of members of Blondie.

One of them was from the English band Silverhead and we chatted about old times and new.

Next day we met Linda in the Village and had breakfast at the Empire Diner, a perfect '30s black 'n' chrome corner café with a long bar, tall stools and a mirror, just the place for a hoodlum shoot out. That evening we met a friend at the Chelsea Hotel, the famous artists and drop-outs colony associated with names like Dylan Thomas. Sid and Nancy threw the Chelsea back into the headlines when I was in New York six months later. The lobby walls were covered in crazy artwork like a Students' Union bar done up for a party.

We had a meal in Chinatown - bright and garish but a bit scruffy as if we had just missed a carnival and the lanterns and tinsel were being cleared away. Then we headed for Christopher Street, all gay bars and shops, mostly clone zones full of denim cowboys and a handful of youths that Clyde knew. The leather bars looked like something from Hammer films, only less camp.

Thursday, 11th May

I packed and left my bags inside the door then Clyde and I caught the subway to the Village once more. I had found a punk hairdresser and decided this was my last chance for dark blue hair. To cut a long story short, I sat for three hours during which everything turned blue – towels, basins, wraps and my scalp.

Everything except my hair, of course, which ended up looking like a purple plastic wig and dangerously abrasive to the touch.

Back at the hotel, everyone was in the limos and Eric was having a fit. No time even to rinse my hair. I gave Clyde a quick, helpless hug and clambered into the car. His thin figure set off down the street with his bag on his shoulder as the car slid out into the traffic.

We headed up through Harlem in the pink light of the setting sun then swung up onto the expressway and over the river. *Goodbye Manhattan*, though the jagged towers were still visible from the airport as lights came on in the dusk.

David had gone on to Paris to dub some vocals for *Gigolo*. The rest of us arrived at J. F. Kennedy Airport, the Americans saying Goodbye to wives and girlfriends. Linda had driven out to see me off and somehow managed to get as far as the first-class lounge without any kind of ticket. I grabbed us a couple of drinks and started to plough my way through a heap of postcards which she promised to post for me. We kissed goodbye and followed the others out to the plane.

I was feeling a bit dazed. The American tour was over. Clyde was over – somewhere on that spiky island. But I am a traveller and here I was with a first-class ticket across the Atlantic. I settled into my seat, dug out a couple of paperbacks and a notepad, ordered a whisky sour. I was right in the nose of the jumbo and as we took off I felt it rise like an elevator. As we levelled out, a steward fixed up my table and spread a white cloth. I started writing to Clyde, but it was just thoughts that never got sent.

After Lincoln limos I'm now experiencing first-class Jumbo treatment. I'm on my second whisky sour and hot canapés. Thinking we're over the ocean, I was surprised to see the lights of a town. We passed Boston on the left a while back, ten minutes after take-off - strange...

NY is alive in my head. Before take-off, I gazed at the Manhattan skyline and tried to picture where you were in relation to the Empire State Building.

They're now serving caviar and Stolichnaya vodka and I'm already feeling more drunk than I can specifically remember being on this tour.

(Later) Watch film about US assault on Everest (successful) - strange seeing people struggle up to 29,028 feet while flying at 33,000!

An hour later with the first hint of light ahead I climbed up the spiral staircase to the bar. Three stewardesses were sitting up there and Dennis was with them. I chatted a bit, gazed out of the porthole a bit. One of the girls went through to the cabin and I had a brief glimpse of a ceiling of little yellow lights.

The clouds ahead formed a false horizon then the sun lifted itself out of this fiery orange layer to become a white incandescent ball. Soon the pilot announced that we were flying over England... but we were heading straight for Frankfurt in Germany. I gazed down at the coast and felt quite homesick. Two months away and another month to go.

9am local time, 3am New York time – and 3am Studio 54 time is no time at all.

CHAPTER 9

GERMANY AND VIENNA

Friday, 12th May

10am on a very grey day, we touched down at Frankfurt Airport. Drove into town between dark fir trees into the bustle of another city – buses, trams, Mercedes. At the hotel, I joined Eric and Tony and Jon from RCA-London for a celebratory beer.

Called my Mum and one or two other people in England then went to bed at 1pm for a few hours (let me see... 7am New York time).

I got up at 5.30pm, washed my hair, changed the voltage on my cassette player, made a few local calls. For most of the past ten years, my group Fumble have been trekking around Europe, especially Germany, and we've made plenty of friends. Suddenly America was behind me and it was great to be back in Germany after a year, looking forward to seeing everyone and very proud to be coming back in style!

I got a taxi to Sachsenhausen, a pretty area of cobbled streets and old buildings on the south bank of the river. Every other door is a café or bar and the streets are full of voluble people strolling around, eating pizzas or wurst. I found the Irish Pub, whitewashed walls, a large open fire and they served draught Guinness. The place is run by Nelli, a lovely girl and a great friend.

She was busy right now, of course, so after a couple of pints of the dark stuff I moved on from Frankfurt's Irish Pub to its American hamburger joint, the Hardrock Café, run by another friend, Cookie. After another club we went back to Cookie's house to play pool and I finally fell into a taxi at 6.30am. I got out at the main railway station and bought some fried chicken then walked back to the hotel in the early morning light, very contented.

Saturday, 3.30pm, Nelli arrived and we walked to an old bar where I had a hearty breakfast then we went for a ride on the Cider Tram - a lovely institution. You squeak and clank through Frankfurt, over the river to the zoo and back sitting at little tables with holes for bottles and glasses, feeling pleasantly mellow.

Then at 7pm it was off to the Festhalle for a rehearsal - mostly making sure all the equipment had survived the flight and the change of voltage. They even flew the grand piano over in a huge triangular flight case!

After that it was another evening of clubs and friends.

Most of the European tour was like this for me - good gigs, good food and meeting old friends. It was great for me but would make rather dull reading so I'll just pick out the interesting and unusual moments.

Sunday, 14th May

The gig went well and I was pleased to know so many friends were out in the crowd.

Monday, we flew to Hamburg. I have covered the hundreds of kilometres of autobahn between these two cities many times, often in a beat-up old van, and I thought back to those days nostalgically as we soared into the sky. Still, if I'm ever back on those roads again I'll be prepared.

Hamburg - Germany's largest port, a beautiful rich city, ancient and modern, with a large yachting lake surrounded by the graceful mansions of ambassadors and industrialists. The sprawling dock area includes Europe's most thriving vice quarter, St. Pauli, with its endless supply of British beat groups.

Fumble first arrived there in a Transit van at 4 o'clock one bitter December morning when the sea was frozen in the harbour. We had half a gallon of petrol in the tank and two marks (20p) in our pockets. We were booked to play at the legendary Star Club and walked nervously up the street, our shivering breath hanging on the air. The sex clubs were open and short, massive bouncers in greatcoats and Hamburg caps shouted at us in half a dozen languages about the girls inside. The Star Club was closed so we sat in the van huddled together under a blanket, while smart young prostitutes smiled in at us and shook their door keys. I got out once to have a piss in an alley and the pool froze before I was finished.

Ten years later, I arrived at the Plaza Hotel in a limousine and stepped out into the fragrant sunshine. All around were beautiful gardens by the lake. Later we drove to the gig which was right next door. I had played here before with Fumble on a tour with Fats Domino – it's a beautiful modern concert hall but only seats 3000.

It was a strange show. A few bouncers stood politely at each side in front of the stage and 3000 smart people sat quietly in their seats – there were no barriers. David, I'm sure, was disconcerted and I think we were all a little nervous. But the people clapped, cheered – and sat tight in their seats. I think there was more action for Fats!

Sometime in the second half, the excitement was obviously too much for one young man in the front row. As David finished 'Ziggy Stardust', he stood up, walked forward to the stage and held up his hand. David shook it and the young man returned to his seat. Wham, bam, thank you, man!

Up in my room I was soon joined by the man who looked after Fumble in Germany. Mostly quiet, sometimes outrageous, he made his money in the streets and clubs of St. Pauli, but he's a likeable rogue. We went to an Italian restaurant on the Reeperbahn then dropped into a couple of bars, catching up with Gerry Marsden and Kevin Keegan, an old friend of Gerry's. At one point we were comparing the popularity of a superstar like Bowie who can fill a stadium for a night with 20,000 people and a football team who can do the same every Saturday.

Next day we were flying to Berlin. At the airport, I noticed a girl crying as we filed through the check-in. Something told me she was crying over David's departure.

Berlin has an air corridor at 10,000 feet instead of the usual 30,000, so the view is what you'd see from a mountain and more interesting than flying above the clouds.

East Germany is mostly flat and dull but at least you feel you're going somewhere. I think I missed the first Wall - the one which runs 2000 miles across Europe from the Baltic to the Black Sea. But I spotted the one around West Berlin, an ugly scar on the green countryside as the Wall is backed by a wide strip of defoliated ground sewn with mines and dotted with anti-tank traps, then a road patrolled by dogs. At intervals there are the stark gun turrets. We crossed this barrier, then swung round and came down at Templehof Airport.

We stayed at the Berlin Hilton, a slightly shabby place on the Ku-damm. My room had a view of the television tower, a silver onion on a tall needle over in the East. The Wall is a makeshift breezeblock construction with a deceptively temporary look.

You can look over into the East and see the desolate no-go area - the tank-traps, concrete crosses that look like rows of fallen gravestones, the harsh lights, the cruel guard towers. In the West you can touch the Wall, in the East you cannot even approach it.

That evening we were all invited out for a meal by Fritz Rau, a large, friendly, bearded man like a Victorian uncle who remembered Fumble from the days when we toured Germany with Bill Haley. We went to a typical Bavarian restaurant, all carved wood, solid tables and bench seats.

David was in a very good mood, recalling some of his bawdier sexploits, exchanging jokes with Dennis. Opposite us was a table of lively Germans. One of them was a very attractive girl with curly chestnut hair.

David called - "Hullo!" and she looked up.

"Do you want to come over here and sit beside me?"

In Germany it is quite normal for a boy to approach a girl who's with another boy - ask her to dance or even to leave her boyfriend (it has happened to us on occasions!) "Me?" she asked. Her English was as meagre as David's German but soon she was sitting next to him.

Back at the hotel I felt a bit at a loss, not knowing anywhere to go, but I was tired and soon fell asleep. Apparently David's girl disappeared soon after they got back so he may have been feeling at a loss too.

Wednesday, 17th May

The Deutschlandhalle was a great cast-iron hangar of a place holding 12,000 but I felt a strange elation to be playing in Berlin.

The gig was pretty controlled, people mostly in their seats, but one young guy was getting excited, jumping about in front of the stage. Near him in the front row was a curious figure like something from a comic opera - middle-aged with blond or white hair, a waxed moustache and neat beard, military looking in a Ruritanian way. I think he was even wearing lederhosen. I don't know who he was, but at a sign from him a couple of bouncers knocked the kid about and started to drag him off. David saw this and waved them away but they took no notice. He shouted "No!" but still they continued, so he stopped the music.

There was an awful silence which surely no one could ignore, but the bouncers carried on and the military man seemed to think this was all part of the show. David ran to the front of the stage just above them. "NO! NEIN! STOP!"

They gazed up at him, suddenly aware they were the focus of attention, then released the youth. David leaned down and shook hands with him - the place cheered. And so, on with the show.

The hotel was dead that night - one or two of the band in the bar but no kids. This is mostly how it was in Europe - when you play Berlin or Paris you could be in any one of a dozen hotels so the kids don't find you - maybe they don't even look. I went out and found a punk place but it was quiet and the barman said everyone had gone to the Bowie gig.

Thursday was Dusseldorf, Friday Cologne, Saturday Munich – more friends, more quiet nights!

★ ★ ★

Monday, 22nd May

We flew to Vienna, the old music capital of Europe. It is one of the few European capitals to emerge unscathed from the last war. Our hotel had probably survived both wars. It had a beautiful marble staircase rising six floors and a rickety old cage-lift running up the middle.

I chose the stairs. My room was papered throughout in brocade with little lamps that looked like candles and probably once were.

We tried to get a late lunch but met a blank – I don't think we went with the furniture. So I found a café selling Viennese cream cakes and with a porcelain pot of hot chocolate in front of me I forgot all about fast food.

That evening we drove past ornate, illuminated façades – theatres, concert halls, museums, palaces and fountains – but we played in a vast gymnasium. As I remembered from the Fats Domino tour it was large and friendly with a heavy echo.

What's your name? name? name? Back at the hotel Dennis

announced he was having a party so we collected up all the booze and trod the wide, faded corridor to his room. Carlos and Simon arrived with some people, whilst Dennis had funky jazz blasting away on the hi-fi. Carlos produced a cassette of the live LP (*Stage*) - it was our first hearing, so partying was quickly forgotten as we eagerly settled down to listen.

CHAPTER 10

FRANCE

Tuesday, 23rd May

Next morning we were off to Paris on an Air France plane. I felt that bubbly Zing! as I stepped on board and said "Bonjour" to the elegant stewardess. Champagne flowed and once we were airborne they served a light French breakfast.

We stayed at the Hotel de la Tremoile, a charming old place just off the Champs Elysées. I offered a round of drinks and more and more tour people kept arriving while I was in the bar, so the bill mounted to a cool £20!

I phoned some friends who invited me round to dinner, so I braved the Paris metro and found my way there up a winding wooden staircase. I enjoyed a delicious dinner and my French came flooding back with the wine. The streets around the hotel were quiet when they dropped me back there and I had a job waking the night porter.

Carlos and I breakfasted together – no one makes omelettes like the French, then we strolled down the Champs Elysées with its fabulously expensive shops and stopped for a beer in a side street. Looking back, it seems strange we didn't see more of what Paris has to offer – the Louvre, the Seine or even the Eiffel Tower – but a city is as much its streets as its palaces and a small bar can be as memorable as a monument.

We had a sound-check at four. The seedy suburbs revealed the Pavilion, a run-down wrought iron cattle market. I ran inside with my camera swinging and got pulled up promptly by a security guard. The place was gloomy with long wooden bench seats. The dressing-rooms were also dimly lit but comfortable. It was typical France – the toilets were disgusting. I have a photo of Dennis in white tennis gear and sola-topi standing by a potted palm like he'd just shot a tiger. Keith Richards came in briefly, looking for David.

We played two nights there – noisy crowd, mixture of very chic and very young. Lots of flowers were thrown and a few fluffy animals. After the show, I met my friend and we all went to a nearby restaurant, a comfortable old place crouching at the end of a cul-de-sac. It was small with a low ceiling and the warmth and smell of good food. I could hardly be further from the noise and hustle of the tour.

Next day, I went looking for boots in St. Germain but didn't find any I liked.

Another night, another show. It was our last night in Paris so David invited us all to The Palace, the Paris equivalent of Studio 54. As we mounted the great staircase, we passed attractive kids who managed to combine a slightly punky look with that touch of Paris style. They nodded a friendly but off-hand greeting to us. After half an hour of noise, heat and scrum-tactics at the bar, I got a taxi back and dreamed of palaces, sidewalk cafés, the Seine, sunshine and the kind of romance not found in a discotheque.

Next day it was back to the shining tubes of Orly Airport. On the plane I sat next to David and Coco, who was clutching a huge, fluffy grey elephant. We chatted a bit and the plane didn't move. Then they announced a delay - they were running off fuel while they changed one of the engines.

"Oh God," David muttered, "that means the pilot's drunk and they're feeding him black coffee."

As we waited, he and Coco got more and more nervous. I think David was on the point of leaving the plane when they told us they were ready - "fasten seatbelts and extinguish cigarettes."

We rolled slowly out across the airport to join the queue of planes at the runway, taking off one by one. Finally it was our turn, the plane poised before the long tarmac strip with its faded paint markings and a thousand black skidmarks. The engines revved and David shifted in his seat beside me. Then we rolled forward as if released down a steep hill, the plane rumbling and wings shuddering as we gathered speed. David was rigid, his hand whitely gripping the arms of his seat. I wanted to hold him tight for comfort but I just put my hand on his arm and felt nearly as tense as he did as the plane threw itself into the clouds.

We drove to the gig through drab dusty streets of big square, white houses with wooden shutters, a typical provincial French town, Lyons. It was Friday and looked like Sunday. The gig was a large, round building with a fluted roof like a dustbin lid. As we approached we slid past a row of dusty, dark-blue police riot-trucks - the ones which feature in so many French gangster films and always seem to be lurking around Paris corners. As we circled the building we passed a large crowd of kids. Later when David arrived, his French driver tried to drop him off in front of the building, right beside the crowd... "I must go back to ze 'otel to collect some more people."

Inside this odd place we found a five-star meal - a fabulous spread of lobster salad, fragrant hot food and excellent wines. The crowd by contrast were the youngest and scruffiest we had seen - they looked like someone else's audience. But they were noisily appreciative and we did a great show. Someone tossed a magazine on-stage for David to sign and during a solo he sat on his heels leafing through it slowly. Every now and then an empty beer can would sail into the air, sometimes falling back into the crowd, sometimes onto the stage – the mood of the crowd was exuberant and stimulating.

The excitement didn't last after the gig. There were no clubs to go to so we just sat in the hotel bar chatting to fans. One guy came up with a striking portrait of David in oils, with the dark hat and bleak expression of *The Man Who Fell To Earth*. He was hoping to get this autographed. David wasn't around but the guy finally got to meet him when we recorded in Montreux.

After an early start next morning, it was a short flight to Marseilles and the Mediterranean. I felt excited as we dropped very low and circled over tiny farms and villages and then the blue sea. We were all in high spirits as we piled into the cars under the hottest sun we had seen since rehearsals in Dallas.

We were soon on a dusty road between white cliffs and the blue sea with dark green palms rustling in the slight breeze. We came into town beside a busy little harbour full of yachts then up a bustling street to our hotel.

I wandered down to the harbour and bought some postcards and a paperback then settled myself at one of the sidewalk cafés for a delicious bouillabaisse (seafood and rice), white wine and a small black coffee.

At the gig, a huge concrete sports hall, the road crew were sunbathing on top of their trucks. Inside, the dressing-rooms were simply an area screened off with canvas. It was comfortable enough but I think we all had in mind that Marseilles had a reputation as a very tough town. Keith Richards told David that the Stones had chairs thrown at them here.

Like Lyons it was a young scruffy crowd but they were noisily welcoming and the show went well – 'Warsawa', "Heroes"… 'Jean Genie'. We had just finished 'Blackout' when there was a sound like speakers farting, then the lights went. For a moment we all stood there stunned, then Carlos shouted "Off-stage everyone!" We covered the space between the stage and dressing-room area under the eyes of the crowd. Eric came in.

"We've got to get out, guys. Where are the cars?"

The cars were out at the back, locked and empty and facing the wrong way. I found the drivers and explained we had to leave – d'urgence! We walked out, casually sauntering to the back exit. David, captain of the ship, came last to give us maximum time before the crowd started to riot.

It was an unpleasant, tense and silent ride back to the hotel. Eric sent us up to our rooms and told us not to come out at all that night. There was a horrible feeling of anti-climax and frustration.

Then Eric called – apparently there was some hope of the gig being saved. It was strange driving back to the hall. There was a roar when we took to the stage and I felt some kind of nervous exhilaration as on the first night. The stage neon lighting rig was dead so everything was lit starkly by the follow-spots out front. It felt like doing a show for the troops just behind the front line - the neons didn't blaze but the music did.

★ ★ ★

Monday, 29th May

We flew up to Bremen in north Germany for a TV show. *Musik Laden* was the largest pop show in the world, going out to all Germany and parts of surrounding countries. The studio is arranged just like a music club with posters of Marx, Dietrich, etc on the painted walls. There's a bar and tables and chairs for 150 kids so the cameras seem out of place, not the crowd.

The stage was quite small and had no barriers but the Germans said there would be no problems. David had put together a short show and we filed out between the scenery and the potted palms to applause from the 150.

They were right about "no problems" - our only problem was adjusting to such a small and self-possessed audience. One girl, who was close enough to reach out and touch David's leg, sat with her back to the stage for the entire performance. Eat your hearts out Bowie fanatics! It was a good show, though.

Next day at the airport we couldn't believe our eyes - the plane was actually square! It was like a large bus with wings and propeller engines. David and Coco were worried about this quaint little monster but I was pleased with anything which broke the jet-setting monotony. We took off for Copenhagen and had a beautiful flight at 10,000 feet with a clear view of little farms and tractors, Dinky cars in Hamburg and ships in the docks. Then we sailed over the gorgeous blue of the Baltic and touched down beside the narrow strip of water separating Denmark from Sweden.

CHAPTER 11

SCANDINAVIA

Wednesday, 31st May

It was a hot afternoon when we checked into our hotel. We were just off the main city square, a large cobbled area dominated by the Radhus, an old red-brick parliament building. Copenhagen is an ancient city, the skyline a jumble of pointed roofs and green copper spires like the opening of a Disney Hans Anderson cartoon.

We were playing two nights here but to only 1500 a night. Soon after we started, when 'Warsawa' was ringing through the hall like a bell chiming the hour, a tall blond gay arrived and seated himself in the front row with such a regal air that he seemed to be granting an audience to David Bowie.

Next morning, I had breakfast at a cheap little restaurant near the station, a Fumble favourite where they do anything from bacon and eggs to chop suey. I spent the afternoon with a friend Pia in the Walking Street and the Tivoli Gardens funfair. After the show we went to a party and a club.

Next day, I heard that David had gone to a big dance hall with a few of the band and had a crazy time playing cowboys and Indians among the crowd. I was sorry we'd missed it as David is hugely entertaining when he's in that sort of mood.

So we flew up to Stockholm, further north than I've ever been. The airport is surrounded by thick pine forests. Recently I came across a bootleg of our show down Portobello Road. It's called *David Bowie Live In Stockholm '79* but of course it's us in Stockholm '78. On the cover you can see my left boot and a hint of my silver jacket behind David's shoulders. One track has a couple of interesting points: in the first instrumental break of 'Breaking Glass' he cries "Hell-God-Baby-Damn!" - our all-purpose Texan exclamation, the catchphrase of the tour. At the end of the song he continues singing *I never touch yoooou...* with a definite Bolan warble. He told me one night he had the strange feeling of Marc's presence at his shoulder - friendly, but it made him shiver.

Next day, I found a shop selling punk clothes, smart and well-stocked with imported gear. I picked out a couple of T-shirts, pink zebra-stripe and a messy green. The girl was just putting them in a bag when something caught her eye.

"Oh, I'm sorry," she said in a precise Swedish accent, "this one has a hole in it."

And she insisted on finding another one, despite my protests.

We flew down to Gothenburg on the south-west coast of Sweden. It was Sunday and the gig went well but the town was dead.

Oslo, capital of Norway, is on a fjord and the airport is right next to the sea. On our way to the hotel we passed four fans from Stockholm sitting on a low wall at the side of the road. They waved as we passed and I noticed that all four of them, two guys and two girls, had bright red hair.

The gig was in a country area, a long sports hall with a curved roof like an aircraft hangar. When we went on-stage, I was amused to see a rash of white-topped sailor caps like the one David wore for an encore. I was surprised people had caught on so fast - then I realised these were all security guys!

I made a few notes later.

Oslo and other shows. People who try to get D's attention for a moment - not to communicate anything but to occupy a brief moment of the Divine Consciousness. I'm amused at the way people suddenly take a photo when they realise he's doing 'Jean Genie' (say) - they want to feel, This is a photo of David actually singing 'Jean Genie'!

People who grab each other as they notice something special - when he drops to one knee or kicks a leg out, crosses his hands like a bird's wings. All his movements are extraordinarily beautiful and none seem without meaning.

David fielding flowers, balloons, etc and getting much applause.

Guy clambers over barrier - David goes forward instinctively to grab his collar so he won't fall.

A guard picks up someone's flowers which fell short of the stage and hands them back for a second try.

★ ★ ★

Tuesday, 6th June

Next day we flew down to Amsterdam, a beautiful city of canals, trams and bicycles.

We stayed there three nights while we played in Rotterdam, the large port 40 miles south. One day I took a tram to the Van Gogh museum, full of vivid paintings and sketches.

The drive to the gig was through flat countryside much like that which Van Gogh painted. The road was lined with straight young trees, behind them pale fields of corn stubble stretching to the low horizon.

The gig was large and the crowd lively after the sedate gig in Scandinavia. It seemed a pity to be driving away from them after the show but Amsterdam was waiting.

Tonight we were being civilised. Carlos, Adrian and I joined David and Coco for dinner in a French restaurant, 'le Bonsoir' – pure luxury after so much inevitable fast food. I asked David how he had put the band together. He had seen

Adrian with Frank Zappa, Simon he had known from the concert scene in the '60s. I couldn't resist asking him about myself – Fumble had supported him in 1973 but I wondered if he had had me checked out since then.

"No," he said, "I just remembered you from before and hoped you hadn't changed too much – you haven't changed at all!" he added with a laugh.

For this tour David had wanted a band which would work as a group, a bunch of people who would gel. He doesn't like virtuosos.

"I'm suspicious of virtuosity," he said, "it doesn't usually go with originality. I like people who have a style of their own."

"Brian Eno had loved the band. He'd love to have done this tour," David told us, 'but he's not strong enough. Both his lungs collapsed on tour once – he just couldn't have taken this.'

We talked about Robert Fripp. Adrian had wanted to call him in New York and David and Coco had been amused at the idea of these two meeting.

"I like talking to guitarists," Adrian announced.

"Frippy isn't like other guitarists," David explained, "he's very introverted."

"Oh, I wouldn't talk shop – I'd just say "Hey! I play an old Strat – what do you play?" then we'd talk about something else entirely."

"Whatever you do," David had warned him, "don't call him Bob."

But knowing Adrian I'm sure he did!

"Frippy has a strange sense of humour," David said.

"So has Adrian."

Later we were discussing which clubs to go to.

"I used to go there a lot with Jim (Iggy) – I think he got beaten up there."

"Oh no!" I made a face.

"Oh that's all right – Iggy seems to get beaten up everywhere."

Friday was the last night in Rotterdam.

Back in Amsterdam after the show, Coco called to say she had got a list of clubs and she and David would be round in a limo.

The first place was on a quiet street and didn't look flashy. Now usually when going into clubs David's identity is revealed to the doorman and we slip in discreetly in a group. But not tonight – David went ahead of us to the door.

"Hullo!" The cockney accent rang out in the dark cobbled street. "Can we come in?" They opened the door, deadpan. I couldn't tell if they had recognised him or not. Inside was a large bar with long tables and benches. The place was pretty full but we managed to grab a table. David and I went to the bar – most of us had beers and the drinks were cheap. Soon we were chatting and looking around at the people.

They seemed very young – all in their teens – and then they were looking at us.

It's funny the way people in clubs react to David. There are the ultra-discos where there's hardly a ripple – everyone is so bored tripping over superstars they can hardly be bothered to pay them any attention. Discreet glances and whispering and a few people say "Hi David!" In the smaller cities, everyone has been to the show and they're all just praying he'll turn up – there you get eager questions and even autograph hunters.

But this place was something else – the kids were doing double-takes, staring open-mouthed and grabbing their friends. We seemed to be in some kind of licensed youth club.

"Time to move, David," I muttered. He hadn't even noticed, hoping to remain incognito by not catching people's eyes. No chance!

David fancied walking to the next place, so the limo followed at a discreet distance nosing its careful way over small humpback bridges. At the next bar, I was first to the door but the guy shook his head. With an apologetic glance at David I explained who we were.

"Yes, but you cannot come in – look..." and he eased the door open a crack against the straining bodies – the place was packed.

A guy spilled out – "I know a place, just a short walk away." We followed him down dark narrow streets, the limo purring behind. Coco's four-inch heels were slipping on the cobbles so I gave her a piggy-back.

Sometimes a bunch of kids would brush past us without a glance then peer into the limo to see if anyone famous was inside.

Then Tony decided to ride and started shouting out to passers by "Hey, that's David Bowie!"

The club was a disaster – bouncers in penguin suits who wanted to charge us to go in – always a bad sign. Coco and I made signs to David but I think he felt he couldn't back out and was delving deep into his pockets for the whole party. So we fled, "See you in Bonaparte's!"

David joined us at this mixed gay club later. We met a few people, talked and danced. As we were splitting for our hotels, Coco complained, "Oh God, I've got to get up early and pack – my room looks like a bomb hit it."

"Haven't you packed yet?" asked David, concerned.

"No darling, I was packing your things for you!"

Brussels, a city of no particular reputation, was chosen as the head of the Common Market. It has some beautiful, ornate buildings, whole untouched squares of them gently illuminated at night. We stayed in a very comfortable modern hotel – Hyatt Régence, one of the American chain.

The show on Sunday night went off as brilliantly as ever to the noisily appreciative crowd. This was an obvious hit-them-and-run gig and the cars surged out of the place as the crowd roar was climaxing after 'Rebel Rebel'. We had an unexpected outrider for this trip – a crazy girl who had followed the tour from Holland appeared on the back of a tiny moped, clutching a crash helmet to her short blonde hair. They provided a kamikaze escort to the hotel where they nearly perished under the wheels of David's limo as it swept in a U-turn to the doors of the hotel.

That night I went drinking with some of the crew - Belgian beers are among the world's best.

The following night was our last in Europe - tomorrow everyone was flying to Newcastle for the first British gig. In the dressing-room someone with a music paper saw Iggy was playing in London tomorrow, so David and I arranged to go.

After the gig, there was quite a crowd already at the hotel entrance when we arrived back, probably people who saw the show last night and now wanted a closer glimpse of the Man. We all swept in through them and I ended up in a lift with David, Tony and Coco. David's face was shiny, his hair a little damp, but still elegant in his white stage outfit and blue dressing-gown round his shoulders. I probably looked like a weekend punk who'd got caught in the rain!

We made arrangements to meet at the Music Machine for Iggy's gig next day.

"Are you going out tonight?" he asked.

"Just for a couple of drinks."

He laughed.

In fact I ended up with a beautiful boy, Jacques, with long red hair. He came back to the hotel with me that night and is the only lover I've ever had who spoke no English.

Of course, the next morning I felt a bit shaky. Jacques and I hauled my cases down to the lobby where I joined Simon's wife Sue and small son Thor, who were catching the same plane to London. We piled our things into a taxi and I turned to say "Adieu" to Jacques. He put his face up and kissed me on the mouth. In a daze, I climbed into the taxi. At the airport I noticed Thor's luggage included a large green balloon and a model of Concorde. When the inevitable BANG! occurred I was glad no security guards came running.

CHAPTER 12

BRITAIN

Tuesday, 13th May

As I emerged at Heathrow, almost hidden behind my trolley of cases, I was met by a bunch of fans plus my Mum. The girls spotted me at once, I'm not sure how. I signed a few autographs and said they should see David in the next few hours – they were rushing about between the three terminals meeting every plane from Belgium!

Back at my flat near Ladbroke Grove I found Mario, Fumble's bass guitarist, and my cat. In my absence the group were all staying there while they did the *Elvis!* show at the Astoria Theatre, so the place was in a state. I cleared a space and flung open my suitcases looking for various presents and souvenirs and all the crazy T-shirts and stuff I had brought back – it was a bit like Christmas!

That evening I met my friend Penny, a zany schoolteacher from Hackney, and went to the *Elvis!* show, surprising people by jumping up for my number (which Barry had taken over). After the show I had a few drinks with the cast then headed up to Camden with some friends. The Music Machine was packed of course, with the 'House Full' notice up. I introduced myself as one of Bowie's band.

"Well, you may be and you may not - I don't know," said the bloke on the door.

"We'll let you in but you'll have to pay."

This seemed fair enough so I shelled out for us all. Later the rest of the group arrived - "Hello - we're Fumble!"

"Oh, good to see you, boys - come on in!"

Inside it was a glorious mass of black-clad bodies. Penny and I managed to squeeze into the elite bar beside the stage and got a few glimpses of the beautiful, primitive Ig.

He wore boots, black tights and a microphone, bathed in a green spotlight, the epileptic contortionist screaming over the relentless backing of his new band. Everyone thought it was very loud but I soaked up the sound happily, very much at home.

It was a tropical wet heat which blanketed the place but there was one cool figure in the bar. In a huge overcoat, collar turned up, was Johnny Rotten, his back to the stage, sucking on a can of beer. His face was dry as an empty talcum tin.

Back-stage I led the way up the familiar narrow stairs to

the firmly closed door, knocked and shouted. "Is that Sean?" cried the Cockney voice and the door opened.

It was dim, dirty and dark like a reptile house, with a few bizarre clothes strewn about the dank floor. On the side there was an open bottle of Jack Daniels, a crate of light ale, a few cokes - no glasses, no ice.

There were a couple of hard chairs with a girl on one of them. David very elegant in a soft green suit and tie, Iggy crouched in a corner peeling off his black tights - a strangely attractive, muscular figure, oily with sweat from head to foot.

"Jim - this is Sean," David introduced us.

Iggy gave a friendly nod and I said something mundane about the show. I introduced Pen, opened a couple of beers for us and leaned against the sink.

Jim in repose is a very different creature from Iggy on-stage. In the manic state of performance his face has the youthful if tortured innocence of The Idiot. Now it was the older, maturer head of a man who has suffered. He talks quietly, earnestly, with an occasional sunny grin.

"I wanted to try out a new mike stand with a ring at the base to stop the lead getting tangled."

"Oh, don't do that," David said in mock horror - "tangled leads are definitely more Iggy."

Someone knocked at the door and announced, "I have a Mr. Rotten here."

David was delighted. "Let him in - oh... is that all right?"

He got up and opened the door. There indeed was Mr.

Rotten in his overcoat, hair on end, face still dry. He had a blonde girl with him who seemed a little wide-eyed at her surroundings. Johnny was soon complaining about the place being too hot, the beer shitty.

"You've dyed your hair," said Jim.

"Yeah, 30p in Woolworths." Soon they were both crouching on the floor in the middle of the room chatting quietly.

Johnny's friend sat on a chair near them.

"So you're a teacher?" said David suddenly from his corner.

Penny started slightly – "Yes" – and soon they were chatting quite freely across the room over the heads of Jim and Johnny. In fact, their conversation seemed much easier as Johnny thought the gig was a load of rubbish and was expecting everyone to agree with him. Coco arrived just then to say the car was ready and Johnny's blonde girl was tugging unhappily at his sleeve. We all got up and made a swift exit leaving Johnny sitting there.

There were two limos outside so David and Jim's party took one and Pen and I found ourselves sailing through London in the vast interior of a Bentley. She was somewhere between gasping and giggles. "I never dreamed anyone would actually speak to me!"

Maunkberry's was one of the top London clubs, fairly trendy. We all sat at a big round table and various people came up to join us or say Hello. The place was practically empty – London on a Tuesday night. We stayed a while then moved to Tramps, just up the road and about the same. Later, Pen and I found taxis and headed off in different directions. My cat was happy to sleep on my feet for the few hours left of the night.

Next day at school, a tired but happy Penny abandoned teaching and sat the kids down – "Guess what I did last night..."

In the morning I taxied out to Heathrow again, timing things so nicely that David and Co. were getting anxious.

"We were worried in case you missed the plane."

"Why, is it the last flight?" I asked.

"The Last Flight!" cried David as if I'd said the Last Supper or something. As we taxied out and revved up they were both as nervous as usual. Coco curled up in a foetal position and put her spiked heel through the plastic cup in the seat pocket in front of her.

We arrived safely. Well, we did – my luggage didn't – it went to Manchester.

"We'll have them up here first thing tomorrow morning," the lady told me reassuringly.

"But I need them tonight," I objected. "I'm appearing on-stage with David Bowie and I've no intention of going on in a pair of jeans!" I'm not used to getting stroppy but this was an emergency. "You'll have to send them up by car straight to the City Hall – that way they'll get here in time." To my surprise they agreed immediately.

Gosforth Park Hotel is an elegant house in its own grounds outside Newcastle – it was now under siege. David was back for his first appearance in two years (Wembley Empire Pool 1976) and for his first tour over here since Ziggy's 'Farewell' in 1973. Some British fans had tickets for every city and had even booked into our hotels. One cheeky youth picked up the house-phone in the lobby and asked to speak to David Bowie – the switchboard girl, obviously missing out on her instructions, put the call straight through!

We drove into town in a coach and had to circle the City Hall a couple of times while police cleared the stage door then we went in in a rush. Five years ago, Fumble had played in this hall supporting David Bowie and the Spiders from Mars. Then it had seemed vast – 2000 seats! Now it looked like a large club – I couldn't believe it.

Behind the stage there was a big, golden pipe organ which looked strange through the neon fence.

The gig that night was amazing. The stage lights reflected from the walls and ceiling lighting up the faces of the whole audience and it looked as if David had invited a crowd of friends along for a wild party.

There was an electric atmosphere, the place seemed to bring performers and crowd together. A balcony ran round three sides of the hall and inevitably one guy jumped down onto an amp, then onto the stage, recovered his balance and made a dash. He threw his arms around David three seconds before Eric and Tony got there then was gently escorted off

132

and back to the auditorium. I think you could say he did it for everyone in the place!

So we romped through two glorious encores and headed for the stage door. "Wait there!" cried Eric, torch in hand, and several of the largest roadies got ready to open the doors. Then all of us, David first, were bundled across the dangerous last few feet separating the stage door from the coach.

There were the usual cries and squeals then the driver eased his way through the kids, some of us waved and we headed out of town for the hotel.

On the way, Pat warned us to be careful of journalists. "There are several staying in the hotel and they'll be trying to get any stories they can."

We stayed in the hotel bar that evening. I felt stimulated to be back in England but I was exhausted and soon went to bed. I didn't meet any journalists.

Next morning I managed to get down while breakfast was still being served. I joined Pat and Tony McGrogan (RCA).

Tony was having the occasional word with a bunch of youths at the next table. They looked a bit punky so I wondered if they were some record company's latest stab at a new-wave band.

I tackled my orange juice then said, "Are you a famous group?"

"No, we're music press - *NME, Melody Maker...*" and they didn't ask me any questions.

We played three glorious nights in Newcastle. Back-stage we had a few visitors including Trevor Bolder, the Spiders' bass player still sporting his long sideburns and Stu, David's 'minder' from those glamourous days. We reminisced about the '73 tours and what we had been doing since. Iggy also joined us and stayed with the tour for a week.

The last night I noticed that Reginald Dixon, the famous cinema organist, was soon to play his farewell concert at the City Hall. I pointed this out to David and at the end of our first half he announced "Now we'll take a short break and Reginald Dixon will entertain you at the organ!"

Saturday, 17th June

Today we were off to Glasgow. The hotel foyer began to get quite frantic as we took our places on the coach. Carlos and I watched from the window taking pictures of some of the stranger fans. Ziggy, whose hair was that familiar flame of translucent pinky-red – with '60s eyes and brows plucked right off, she might have been the alien's younger sister. Ian was another celebrated lookalike with a striking profile. Another girl had green-flash hair – "One day", Carlos told me, "she and Ziggy got a lift in David's car and she was sick all over the place!"

Now David was coming through the lobby, surging towards us amidst a lively group of people, some waving pieces of paper. Stu and Leroy were at his shoulder but Iggy was on the edge of all this, unnoticed and unconcerned.

The trip to Scotland was idyllic. The weather was fine and much of the scenery on the coast road was breathtaking. Most of the band had wives, girlfriends and even young kids along with them and the coach was like a holiday outing. David was relaxed and happy.

We stopped at a pub on the road. It was quiet inside with just a few locals who didn't pay us any attention. Some of them did pass comment on Iggy, visible outside in bright green jeans. Then we were just on the point of leaving when the barmaid, Doreen, grabbed David's arm.

"Aren't you David Bowie?" she asked eagerly and dragged him round the bar introducing him to the puzzled locals – more like a long-lost cousin than a pop star. In the normal way, Tony or Eric would have intervened but today was a holiday and we all piled happily into the coach to wait until Doreen emerged with David, giving him a big kiss before releasing him. We all cheered as he joined us, grinning. A few minutes later we crossed the border.

"Break out the kilts!" someone shouted and I tried to imagine our hero in one.

As we drove to Edinburgh, we saw half-a-dozen skydivers trailing coloured smoke across the blue. We visited the castle like a coach-load of real tourists and I have a nice snap of Iggy in his green jeans standing beside a large cannon.

The hotel in Glasgow was in the middle of town, smart

and comfortable and immediately besieged, although David was staying just out of town somewhere. Over the next few days the hotel lounge and bar were constantly occupied by groups of our crowd, RCA people, MAM people (the tour promoters) and fans who had booked in, sneaked in or been invited in by one of the party. I spent most of the time trying to write – I had started on this book but it was slow progress. It was odd, the British tour provided most of the wildest gigs but between times was deadly dull. One evening someone suggested I should chat up Ziggy who was always around in the bar, but I said I don't think I could handle coming down to breakfast with someone who looked like David in '73.

Monday was our first Scottish gig. It was early afternoon when we arrived at the theatre but already there were kids milling about and the lane beside the theatre leading to the stage door had a few policemen at each end to keep it clear.

The Apollo Theatre is an extraordinary old building, tall, rambling and full of dingy atmosphere, and we were soon making jokes about *The Phantom Of The Opera*. The theatre holds 300 with two balconies. Five years ago when we played here the top balcony was closed as unsafe. Now it had been strengthened and was open. I went up there gingerly to have a look, finding my way up through the labyrinth of dark passages and stairs. The balcony was so high and steep I wanted crampons. Far below was the stage and the rig. The neons were flashing and the whole contraption looked eerie, like Victorian sci-fi.

That night was Eric's birthday which was celebrated back-stage with a large haggis and a Scots piper in full dress. I got chatting to Jim (Iggy) and we found we both liked browsing in the Portobello Road for old books of Victorian travels, etc.

Another evening before the show I slipped out of the theatre to a nearby fish 'n' chip shop for white pudding and chips followed by a pint of *o'heavy* and a whisky chaser in a nearby pub, just as I had done five years ago. We played four nights in Glasgow and those shows are now a glorious blur but I do know that all of them were sensational.

When Scotland loves you, they let you know it! Later I heard a bootleg cassette which has more excitement than any show I've ever heard.

The atmosphere was electric already and burst around us when we appeared.

Throughout 'Warsawa' there was barely suppressed hysteria which kept breaking out into screams and little bursts of applause and shouting. When Dennis's drum phrase triggered the first chords of "Heroes", the dam burst and everyone was clapping along with the number and indeed through most of the show.

At one point the unbelievable happened and a young guy threw himself at the front of the stage and began to climb, over barriers, cables and lights, a twelve foot assault. Eric and Leroy ran forward... to help him up! "I was afraid he'd kill himself falling into the lights," said Eric later.

We came on for the second half, David introduced the band and we crashed out the first chord. *Pushing through the market square...* (HOORAY!!!) By the time we came to *telephone, opera house, favourite melodies,* they were singing along with him. Now they were louder than David. He mimed with his hands. He struck a pose which reminded me of Nureyev taking an encore...

At the end of 'Star' he shouted *Watch me now!* on the last chord, the only time I remember him doing this.

At the end of 'Ziggy Stardust' when he sings *But Ziggy played...* in that pause, the crowd joyously sang *GUITAA-AR!* and Carlos, grinning widely, played the last chord, letting them steal the ending from David. The cheer that followed broke into screams as Adrian ground out the first notes of 'Suffragette City'. The crowd clapped and stomped and the place shook. I looked up and was horrified to see the whole structure of the top balcony was bouncing at least twelve inches to the beat. The spotlights up there were waving their long beams, amplifying the movement of the floor. I shuddered, imagining the carnage if anything gave way. WHAM BAM THANK YOU MA'AM!

The next two numbers, 'Art Decade' and 'Alabama Song' were a relief, allowing people to take a breather before the final burst.

As Roger's steam train invaded the place, the yellow-white lights placed in the shiny black stage chased strange shadows around the theatre. I leaned against a speaker at the side of the stage. David came over and joined me.

"I think for Earls Court I'll have a model train running to and fro along the front of the stage."

I didn't look to see if he was grinning...

It's not the side effect of cocaine... and as the lights blazed forth the crowd sang back to him *I'M THINKING THAT IT MUST BE LOVE!* And it was, on both sides.

"Thank you! We thank you!" And we dashed off till the shouts of "WE-WANT-BOWIE" brought us back for 'TVC15'. Then off again, more shouts, Dennis leads the band back, banging a cowbell, into 'Stay'. At the end, two bars of cowbell and straight into 'Rebel Rebel' which raised a bigger shout than ever. Then "We will see you next year..."

"Bye! - Sean Mayes - Simon House - Carlos Alomar - Daniel Davis - George Murray - Roger Powell - Adrian Belew - David Bowie - Thanks!"

That was the end. Down to the stage door, quick look out, David into his limo, then our coach squeezed up to the door, we piled in, off up the alley, the police parted and we drove out.

Flashback to 1973: When Fumble supported David, we were delighted with the gig but pissed off at the security - the whole back-stage area was taken for David and entourage, part of the Defries build up of Bowie mystique. We were given a room out front and had to reach the stage through the auditorium, guitars in hand.

Once on-stage we were happy. It was an amazing gig, the

audience roared like an earthquake - the thunder of adrenalin. We even got an encore, and left the stage drenched. But now what? We just couldn't walk back through the auditorium and the crowd ("Four ices, please miss!") so the only way was the stage door and round the outside.

We emerged from the stage door running - it was January and we were soaked - and found ourselves in a small alley. Now David was quite a big star and the show was a sell-out, but there was no hysteria surrounding the place like today... there were two girls and one young policeman. As we appeared, the girls squealed. The copper suddenly realised here was his moment of glory and he thrust his arms out holding back the girls.

We ran past laughing and thought, if only the press could show this scene of fan hysteria outside Mr. Bowie's concert!

Next day it was down to Birmingham by coach again, but David was going by train and asked me if I'd like to come along. Five minutes after I reached the station I saw several familiar figures coming towards me.

David was obviously incognito, wearing a chunky white fisherman-knit pullover (souvenir of Scotland), roughly rolled-up blue canvas bags, dark glasses and an unlikely tweed cap. He had his head down and was casting furtive glances about him.

We passed through the barrier, an old guy clipping our tickets. "There you go, David - good show I heard, sorry I missed it," - deadpan. And I was trying not to laugh as we boarded the train.

"Nice cap, David," I said.

"Oh thanks, do you like it? Someone threw it on-stage last night."

We settled ourselves in a first-class compartment, David, Coco and me, with Rob and Leroy as escort. It all seemed very easy and peaceful. But we soon realised a few unsuspecting fans were on the train themselves. A French youth was the first to spot us and he quietly presented David with a fluffy toy pig, *la Gigolo*. He accepted it cheerfully.

We soon went along to the restaurant car.

One or two fans passed us without noticing – they were usually running. David and I were sitting next to the aisle. Then one kid saw me.

"Hey, you play with David Bowie, don't you?"

"Yes, that's right." (Trying to keep a straight face.) "It was a great show last night."

"Thanks – are you going to Birmingham too?"

"Yes, I've got tickets for the whole tour, not every show but every... oh...er, oh!"

"Hello David-er-Mr-Bowie!"

"Hello."

"We didn't know you were going by train."

"Oh yes, I like trains."

He gave an autograph and the fan rushed off.

After lunch we looked through a picture punk book Roger had given me (I looked right through the pile for a scruffy copy but they were all mint!) and conversation turned to Johnny Rotten. Coco hadn't met him before the Iggy gig in London and didn't like him.

Rob knew Johnny and Sid quite well from the time when he'd been looking after Iggy.

"They used to follow him everywhere when he was touring over here. Jim didn't seem to mind most of the time. Johnny had this big bodyguard – he would appear at Jim's door in the hotel and say "I've come for Iggy," and poor Jim, he'd be huddled behind the door shaking his head. I didn't think much of Johnny but Sid was interesting to talk to, if you could stand the smell."

Later, when we were back in our apartment, one of the kitchen staff put his head in. "Excuse me, Mr. Bowie, I hope you enjoyed your meal and I wonder if the staff could have a few autographs?"

"Not just now – perhaps a bit later."

"Well, we thought maybe..."

"No," said Coco sharply, "he doesn't want to be disturbed."

"Oh, I see," said the young man and left slamming the door.

Leroy was up in a flash and followed him. He was back again in a couple of minutes.

He says, "Sorry, you won't be disturbed again," he announced.

Bingley Hall is nearer to Stafford than to Birmingham, right out in the country. It's a great hangar of a place where I believe they hold cattle markets. Outside was a queue – can you imagine 8500 people queuing? I felt sorry for them as they shuffled between barriers in a continuous crowded line from the car park, round three sides of a football pitch and along the side of the hall. The sky was overcast but not actually wet.

We played three nights there and the shows were great. David really enjoyed it. I had some friends up there so I stayed with them the first two nights. It was strange to watch the coach rush off after the gig. The next day we went to a wine bar and though it felt a bit unreal it was good to relax away from the tour 'circus'.

The second night after the show there was a party for the crew like the one I missed in Los Angeles at The Forum. They had a disco and some strippers, stage style but in danger of falling flat. Then Dennis took over the mike while the strippers were on and gave a hilarious fashion show commentary. At first the girls were a bit put out but soon got the joke and played along.

The evening's top performer was a beautiful black woman and later she joined David at his table.

A few fans managed to get in through a kitchen window and mingled happily with the crowd.

CHAPTER 13

LONDON

Tuesday, 27th May

We left Birmingham by coach that morning. It was strange to be driving down that old familiar route, the M1. Soon the coach was nosing through the London traffic, easing past big red buses, and some of the Americans were getting their first glimpse of London. Finally we crawled down Park Lane to the Inter-Continental. I checked in with the rest - my flat was in such a state I decided to spend the week in the hotel!

That night I went to see the *Elvis!* show again with Ron. He enjoyed it and even thought the American accents weren't too bad!

The following night I met up with Rob and a girl in the hotel bar. He's big and confident and has worked for David for some years.

"I've seen musicians come and go like changing your socks."

I told him I was surprised when David contacted me and sometimes felt a bit inadequate as the others are more typical high-powered instrumentalists than me.

"You're what David wants," he said, "and you can really play that mother."

I also learned more about Moose, who's quiet and casual but saved the gig in Marseilles when the PA blew up. "He has a degree in maths", Rob told me, "and used to be a trouble-shooter for IBM. If one of their computers got sick, he'd fly in and sort it out."

"Oh no, I asked him to fetch me beers when we're practising!"

"Yes, but that's OK, we're all here to do whatever's got to be done."

He talked a bit about Iggy. "David got this idea Iggy was in trouble so he sent me out to LA to find him. Well, he was in this room with a crowd of jerks, all crazy types lying around out of their heads. And Iggy, God's truth, he was sprayed all over with paint. I hauled him out. 'What the fuck are you doing? You'll kill yourself!' So after that, I hung around with him on tour, and I had to teach him to be Iggy on-stage and Jim off. And some nights I'd be picking glass out of his back and pouring on alcohol after the show."

Thursday, 27th June

D–Day: It was raining gently as we drove along Kensington Road beside the Park. After Cadillacs and Mercedes we were now resplendent in a Rolls, a Bentley, and an Austin Princess. London looks different from the back of a Rolls! Soon the ugly humped shape of Earls Court Stadium loomed into sight with its crowds of costumed acolytes. We drove up a long ramp at the back between two guarded gates then into the back of the hall, a vast parking space where the three huge trailers were tucked away in a corner. Later on I counted seven limousines parked alongside the trucks. I took a photo of them all lost in a small corner of the back-stage area. That is Earls Court.

Four trailer caravans were drawn up in a square like a small camp, the floor between them astro-turfed with a ping-pong table, large potted plants and a few chairs. I dumped my bag in our room then climbed the dozen steps to the stage.

I don't think Earls Court was quite the biggest gig – Madison Square or the LA Forum may have been bigger. But for me, Earls Court was the one. It was vast and awe-inspiring. I gazed at it from the stage. Then I went down and looked up at the stage from below.

Back-stage people were arriving – wives, girlfriends, kids playing ping-pong or fighting. The atmosphere was relaxed and cheerful. But as the time grew near and we could hear the great hall filling up, I realised I was a little nervous for this one. There were quite a few friends coming, and this was London and a biggie. Then Coco looked in.

"Sean, Simon, could you wander over in a few minutes and have a word with poor David? He's terribly nervous! Don't mention I said anything."

So, drinks in hand, we went over to David's caravan. It was the usual scene - a table of food and drink, a magnificent display of flowers, the rack of clothes, three-quarter mirror on a stand, ironing board in the corner. David did seem pleased to see us as we said this and that. There we were, David a little quieter than usual, me a little bouncier, Simon deadpan, but the three Londoners of the group were each nervous to be facing a home crowd.

But once on-stage it was fine, for me at any rate, and for David, too, I'm sure. The pre-show nerves just pushed my excitement higher. Des, Fumble's singer and guitarist, had gone 'sick' from the *Elvis!* show that night (everyone is covered) - this was something he couldn't miss. He felt a burst of pride and a kind of amazement as I ran out on-stage - I was the first (as I had to cross the stage to the piano) and it seemed as if the 15,000 were cheering for me!

It was another small riot of a show. Hell, it was *the* riot of a show with people singing, clapping, jumping, climbing on their seats, kamikaze kids rushing the barriers. The fascinated sexual gaze of the front rows, bathed in stage light, made it hard to breathe at times. There came a moment when the security guys gave up the struggle and leaped behind the crash barriers just below the stage, so from there back it was a sea of humanity – *It's too late!* ROAR!!!

'Rebel Rebel' – bounce bounce – and off into the purring limos for the triumphal procession back through the lights and wet streets of London.

Friday afternoon we went very early to Earls Court. Tonight the show was being filmed by David Hemmings (director of *Just A Gigolo*) for a general-release feature. Inside there was all the paraphernalia involved – trucks, generators, a giant crane arm behind the stage to lift the cameraman right up over the rig. Tony Visconti was here, very cheerful in a bright red T-shirt. As we played, they checked camera angles – my hands on the piano, shot along the keyboard, and David Hemmings even wanted one of me leaning against an amp swigging a can of beer.

It was another mind-blowing show that night but as soon as the gig was over I jumped into a taxi and headed for Camden – I had got another gig! At Dingwalls I met Fumble hotfoot from the *Elvis!* show.

"Rhythm 'n' booze" is the club motto so I got a crate of beer and installed it in the dressing-room with a bottle of Jack Daniels from the gig. Things soon became hectic.

Even a normal Fumble gig at Dingwalls is like a party but tonight was really crazy.

The usual busy Friday night crowd was bursting with friends. *Elvis!* people and tour people. Word had got around so there were also Bowie fans and Elvis fans, some so young they couldn't come in but stood outside the stage-door, which was thoughtfully open as the club was so hot.

It was a lively joyous gig, though not one of our most controlled! About the third number there was a stir as the Bowie party arrived. Des told me afterwards that when he saw David he could hardly sing for nerves. Later some of the *Elvis!* people joined us on-stage and we finished with a couple of encores.

"I'd like to thank David for lending us a piano player!" Des announced to laughter and cheers.

Afterwards David joined us in the tiny dressing-room.

"I really enjoyed that," he said, opening a can of beer. "I loved 'C'est la Vie' and the Gene Vincent number."

It was such a squeeze in there we were worried about David's voluminous brown suit getting creased.

"Oh, don't worry," he said with a laugh, it's meant to be like that - it's my Crumpled Suit."

"Yes, it's such a shame," Coco told us, "tonight the dear old lady who looks after the place produced it on a hangar and said, 'I had such a job ironing this for you!'"

David Hemmings had invited us all down to the Alibi Club in the King's Road so we were soon relaxing in more comfortable surroundings. Des's wife and son were with him. It was Tyson's eleventh birthday so he had come along as a treat – he hardly ever gets to see his Dad play. Back in '73 he got into trouble at school for making up stories. When asked, "What does your father do?" he said. "He's playing guitar in America with David Bowie!"

With his blonde hair he reminds me a little of Zowie and tonight he was in his element. He sat right next to David and they swapped jokes, a performance much funnier than the jokes themselves.

We finally left when dawn was breaking and birds were singing in the trees of Sloane Square.

Saturday, 1st July

Last day of the tour. I went over to Pat's hotel, a beautiful and discreet place near Marble Arch. He had a large suite with a spiral staircase leading from the lounge to the bedroom. We sorted out what money was due and I walked out of the place nervously with £2,000 in cash.

That night at Earls Court everyone was in very festive mood. There were a few film cameras backstage grabbing incidental material. David arrived with Bianca and one of the cameras swung their way, but Pat shook his head to that shot.

When we were sound-checking, I noticed a bystander wearing a sensational red sweat-shirt with Red Indian designs. Penny had asked me to get her an American baseball shirt and I had bought one or two but nothing really special. This one I had to have.

"Well, I'm not keen to part with it," he drawled, "but I'm looking for some cash to buy coke."

I worried about the ethics as I stuffed the prize in with my stage gear.

I had twenty people on the guest list that night. Mario, Fumble's bass player, brought his camera but got a seat where I was hidden by the PA! Penny came and so did my Mum. Pen saw her in the crowd at the box office. My Mum gave her name and the girl looked through her list.

"I'm afraid your name isn't here," she said without much interest. "Perhaps he forgot to put you down – there are so many names."

"I doubt if he has forgotten," said my Mum firmly, "my son is David Bowie's pianist."

The girl looked up startled, and soon found the name on another sheet. Then my Mum nearly gave the ticket away to someone else who was having difficulty getting one!

My Mum was very impressed with David and the band, though rather overwhelmed by the crowd and the volume. She got into conversation with two girls sitting next to her who were surprised to see someone of my Mum's generation at the show and were delighted when they found out why.

The gig was sensational, the final high of the tour. The

surge to the front started almost immediately so we played to a seething crowd of excitement. The first half was magnificent, the second just wild.

During the second encore, a kid in the crowd threw his sailor hat to David, who took off his own and put it on, then he came over and put his cap on my head at a careless angle.

As he turned back, Leroy appeared with an armful of caps and David handed them out.

As 'Rebel Rebel' ended he threw his cap into the crowd and we all did the same as we ran off. (Penny was out there praying, *Sean, please don't throw yours!*) This time we didn't dive into the cars - David wanted to go out again.

"What can we do?" he wondered. "Can anyone remember 'Sound And Vision'?"

So that night, and no other, we played 'Sound And Vision', the ridiculous Mantovani strings singing over the rapturous crowd, and I was taken back to a night a year ago in a bar in Copenhagen when I heard this playing and wondered if David ever remembered a group called Fumble and a piano player called Sean.

Back at the hotel my friends started arriving. Pen was one of the first and I produced the sweat-shirt I had bought earlier.

"It's enormous," I said. "You'll probably have to alter it, and it hasn't even been washed."

No matter - she immediately tried it on and it looked like a short dress over her footless tights.

"This is what I'm wearing tonight!" she announced. "I won't meet anyone wearing the same!"

My room was soon crowded with people I hadn't seen for months. They squeezed in where they could and helped themselves to drinks. In the middle of all this the phone rang and Carlos told me David was going to Tramps and all the band plus girls were invited to join him. That was awkward – Tramps was unlikely to let all my crowd in but I didn't want to snub David by not turning up. I decided we would try, with another club in reserve, which is where we ended up.

But first we ran the gauntlet of crowds in the hotel lobby who wanted to know "Where's David?" and "What's happening?" One crazy looking girl I had noticed in the front row rushed up and asked me to take her along. "You should get in without any trouble," I told her.

"Why?" she asked.

"Aren't you Cherry Vanilla?" (who did publicity in the New York Mainman office back in Ziggy days.) "No," she said.

"Well, tell them you are at Tramps and you'll get in all right." (And she did!)

I had a great time with my friends down at The Royalty, a club for actors and musicians where you could dress up or down, pose or relax, dance or talk. It was reasonably cheap and a favourite haunt of the boisterous *Elvis!* crowd. We met more friends there including an American who told Pen she was wearing a Chicago Black Hawk shirt.

When The Royalty closed at 2am, I said "Goodbye" to

everyone then Pen and I headed back to Tramps. A crowd of kids were still hanging around the entrance.

There were stairs leading down into the club and in front of us a girl at a desk. As we entered a handsome black guy came up the stairs and walked out - it was Arthur Ashe, the tennis star. Pen squeezed my hand without saying anything.

The girl at the desk told us no one else could come in. As I explained who I was she said I was the third David Bowie pianist to show up that night and she was letting no one in. I could tell she had had a full night but this was getting silly. While I was pondering a familiar couple came up the stairs - David and Bianca.

"Hullo, David," I said, "I'm having a little trouble getting in."

"Oh, he's kosher!" David called out to the girl.

Downstairs it was crowded and smoky and the clamour seemed equal parts chatter and music. Penny and I joined Carlos and his beautiful wife, singer Robin Clarke.

David returned after seeing Bianca to her car but this was one of those occasions when everyone wants to talk to him, so we stayed clear. The place was very lively. In the loo, Penny ran into a crowd of deb-y girls in Red Indian fancy dress. They looked suspiciously at her while pouring Channel No. 5 over their cool shoulders.

Later on we talked to David Hemmings about filming, the '60s, the tour, etc.

Finally we walked up Piccadilly trying to hail a cab for Pen.

"Do you remember one thing David Hemmings said about David – that he's such a joy to film because he moves so well, so naturally. I once heard John Arlott say there's no one in cricket as graceful as Gary Sobers – no matter what he was doing, batting, fielding – even just walking out to the wicket."

Another taxi went by.

"You know, I think I'll write to *Jim'll Fix It* and ask him to make a film of David and Gary walking together," she said, "the two most beautiful walks in the world."

That was the last night of the American/European tour but there was one more thing to do before everyone flew out. Next day, Sunday, we went to Tony Visconti's tiny studio in Dean Street to record 'Alabama Song'. It had been such a hit on the tour that David wanted to do it as a single.

It was an interesting process. David had some new ideas for the drumming. He wanted Dennis to play very freely against the rhythm to give an unstable, insane atmosphere to the track. When we tried to do this it proved hilariously difficult so we finally laid the backing down without drums then Dennis overdubbed his demolishing attack when his efforts couldn't disturb the beat.

David had us record several verses and choruses which he edited together later in the order he felt worked best.

I think the final result is interesting but not completely successful – I prefer my two bootleg versions!

Footnote - the film of Earls Court is still lying in the vaults.

CHAPTER 14

LODGER

August/September

I threw a 'Welcome Home' party two weeks after that last hectic Saturday night and of course told my friends about the tour. But I soon learned that life was simpler if I didn't mention the Bowie connection when meeting people – disbelief would be followed by a barrage of questions. So I'd just say I played with a rock 'n' roll band Fumble – had they ever heard of us? For the first time in my life I felt pretty well-off. I bought a couple of cameras, a pocket one for fun and a Pentax with a big zoom lens.

Then early in September I flew to Geneva. Simon and I were driven to Montreux in blistering sunshine. It's a forty mile run round the north of the lake.

On our right was the glistening water backed by the

French Alps, on our left the vineyards rising gently to lower mountains.

This is a part of the world I know well from Fumble's trips and I felt exhilarated to be back.

Mountain Studio is right on the lake. We stepped out of the car to see a familiar group of figures lounging in the sun.

David had a crew cut and needed a shave.

He looked drawn but alert, gave us a quick hug of welcome then we went into the cool elegant Swiss control room. Gleaming equipment, thick pile carpet, rough stone walls, very chic. Three small TV screens gave a fragmentary impression of the studio itself – drums, mike stands, Carlos tuning an acoustic guitar.

David had chosen the intimacy of a small studio up a winding stairway. Here there was little space between the screened amps and the piano was blanketed by a huge white fur carpet which cascaded to the floor like mountain slopes.

Tony Visconti was at the mixing desk, cheerful and relaxed as usual – he always creates an easy atmosphere in the studio, helping to relieve the tensions which can arise.

David had been working for a few days with Carlos, George and Dennis laying down rhythm tracks. They were just roughly mixed with occasional ideas for vocals. David sat there, his eyes bright, sometimes singing a bit – 'Yassassin'! 'Red Sails'! – and telling us the instrumental lines he wanted here and there. They all had working titles – 'This Tangled Web', 'Portrait Of The Artist', etc but none of these survived onto *Lodger* – and even this title lay unthought of at the time. David was working from the bottom up and would complete the backing here in Switzerland before he wrote any of the lyrics. He did that in New York early the following year after the end of the Far East tour.

Before we left that day we all had a short jam on one of the chord sequences he had in mind. We finished quite early and went back to the hotel. This was a big old-fashioned place, typical of Montreux. My room was large and comfortable with a balcony and a beautiful view of the lake and the mountains. We had dinner in the hotel that night then chatted in the bar. It rained heavily.

Carlos was his usual beaming self and he looked younger now he had shaved off his thin moustache. He told me that Roger was unlikely to be playing on the LP. This album was to be the last of a trilogy (with *Low* and *"Heroes"*) involving Brian Eno in concept, composition and performance, so two synthesiser players were not needed. But I missed him. It felt strange for the band to be incomplete. I wrote him a line to keep in touch and say I was sorry we wouldn't be seeing him.

Next morning I had breakfast on the balcony. The studio was a pleasant ten minute walk away beside the lake. Over the next couple of days we laid down a few more basic tracks. David or Brian would provide the chord sequence, often quite a short one, and we would play this over and over continuously. These sequences were produced by various methods, sometimes almost at random. On one occasion Brian wrote out a collection of cards with chords on them - B flat, F, C, E, G, E flat, A minor, C minor - then pinned these on the wall and, giving us a basic rhythm, pointed to them with a baton while we played. There was some grumbling about this 'back to school' session!

At the end of the day, Tony would run off rough mixes of everything onto quarter inch reel-to-reel for David and Brian to take away, listen to and cut up. The next day they would be back with the spliced tapes, often loops, then these edited versions would be reproduced by splicing and looping the multi-track and copying it. I'm not sure now which tracks of this album contain loops but an obvious example from before is 'Blackout' where the whole song is built on two basic structures over which the vocals create three distinct sections.

This method of writing seems to work because David has such a strong sense of tune. He has a way of producing vocal lines which spring from the roots of the music, something which I noticed on tour when he recreated each song every night often varying the vocal line as if the songs were alive and growing.

David was very keen on spontaneity. He liked everything to be recorded in one or two takes, mistakes and all. Often when he chose a section for looping he would pick the part with the most mistakes, which when repeated became an integral part of the song. Sometimes the approach would be light-hearted, almost frivolous. (Historical note: 'Jean Genie' was recorded in a single take and you can clearly hear a mistake – someone not quite sure which bit comes next just before the first chorus!) On one occasion everyone swapped instruments – Tony on bass, George on drums, Carlos on organ I think, and Brian on piano. The track became the single 'Boys Keep Swinging'. Another time someone was sent to the local music shop to borrow three mandolins which Adrian, Simon and Tony strummed on 'Fantastic Voyage'.

A few days after I got there all the basic tracks were down and Carlos, George and Dennis flew back to New York. Then Adrian, Simon and I would alternate in solo sessions in the studio while the others played frisbee in the gardens outside. These sessions were pretty intense. I would sit at the piano, Tony in the control room, and David would run up and down between us humming ideas. On 'Move On' for instance, he wanted a grandiose theme, "something like Dvorak" he prompted. Every number was dispatched quickly and by the end of the day I was left with no clear impression of anything I had played. They only came back to me again when I heard the finished LP six months later!

We worked fast and I was through just five days after I arrived. I made a few diary notes on the last day.

Take a huge sandwich to the studio, consume in sun till people arrive. Brian plays through a tape he's been editing ("Here we go loop-de-loop," hums Tony) "Put on 'Fury'," says David.

"That was 'Occident Prone'," - Tony. *"What a terrible pun!"* -
Brian. *"That was Brian's"* - David*. "Yes I'm sorry,"* says Brian,
"I've been playing with words again."

Finally, *"See you in Sydney,"* says David.

That night I went out with Simon and Adrian, Pat and his
wife Peggy. She and I were discussing how David looked
with very short hair and several days' growth of beard.

"Yes, I called at his flat in Berlin just after he'd had it cut,"
she said. "I saw this scruffy unshaven man lying on the floor
in a pair of overalls and thought it was a plumber!"

Next morning, Saturday, I saw Pat to sort out the
arrangements for the second half of the tour. We were
starting in Australia in November so I asked him if I could
fly via New York and LA. He said fine - I could join up with
the party flying out from Los Angeles.

I felt elated as I left the hotel. I was now starting a real
holiday right here in Switzerland. At the station I caught the
narrow-gauge train which winds its way up into the mountains.
I stayed with friends in an old chalet halfway up a mountain
- a complete change from touring and from London.

As a postscript to the album, in March 1979 David took
the tapes to New York where he wrote all the words in a
week, working at a white heat inspired by the city.

He did some more work with Adrian - the end of one
track consists of three guitars playing on separate tracks
mixed in and out, David playing with the sliders like a video
game. He also used Roger on 'Repetition': "Can you make

à sound like bodies falling behind doors?" I spent three beautiful, relaxing weeks up in the mountains and saw the first snow of a winter I would soon leave behind. Then I flew to New York and stayed with Carlos and his family high up in a block near Central Park. I went to see Clyde in Philadelphia then flew to Los Angeles, staying with Art, who lives on Hollywood Boulevard right in the middle of things. I loved the palm trees and the ocean and Little Venice where half the kids were on skates.

After ten days in LA a white limo wafted us to the airport and we were back on tour again. It was Thursday evening, 2nd November, 1978.

CHAPTER 15

AUSTRALIA

Thursday, 2nd November

A few minutes after 10pm we walked out onto the tarmac and mounted the steps to the plane in the warm Californian evening. Soon we were toasting the tour in champagne then we took off over the Pacific and I thought, *Now I'm further west than I've ever been.*

Nine hours later we saw the first signs of dawn. We dropped through the clouds into the darkness below for the first of two stops - I didn't know where. I caught glimpses of beach and surf, mountains, harbour lights. As we stepped off the plane the heat hit us. It was unbelievably hot and damp like a sauna, with a caramel smell like burning wood. I grinned with delight as I caught sight of the name TAHITI on the building.

But all Tahiti had to offer was a three-hour wait in the clammy airport lounge. We swigged ice-cold Heineken and watched the sun rise over steaming vegetation outside. I sent a few postcards - *Tahiti!*

At last we took off again. Breakfast. We were over halfway, crossing the infinite Pacific, magic islands floating past below us, white beaches and jade water. We landed briefly on Fiji, bought T-shirts, sent more postcards, took off again. Breakfast.

We came in over Sydney harbour ("There's the Bridge! Look, the Opera House!") at 4pm Saturday, having crossed the date-line and lost a day - which looks odd in my diary! We walked into the hotel feeling tired and dirty. It's springtime in Sydney and tomorrow is November 5th. It didn't seem quite real.

The Sebel Town House is an attractive hotel, the staff friendly and everyone has a good time. They were having a pretty good time when I arrived - Tony McGrogan was celebrating the start of the tour with the crew and local tour people. I joined them and forgot to feel tired and dirty again until I crashed in my bed late that night.

David and Co. arrived a couple of days later. I stepped into the lift one morning, joining Coco and a few other hotel guests.

"Hullo," I said to her, "have you just arrived?"

"No, we flew in last night."

"Is his Lordship still asleep?"

Coco laughed and nodded at someone beside her. It was

David – we were face to face and I had completely missed him! He was very amused but I felt a complete fool. "I must be the one who's still asleep!" I sometimes wonder if he has learnt the eastern art of invisibility in a crowd.

We rehearsed for a week in a small indoor sports stadium. One morning the road was blocked by a giant crane installing floodlights for the football ground next door. I was amused at the name of the firm – The MEN from MARRS.

On Thursday after our last rehearsal, I joined David and Stu and a girl in the limo. A minute later we had a flat tyre.

"Let's go in there," said David, so while the driver changed the wheel we all piled into a smart hotel bar across the road. They didn't look too pleased at our slightly scruffy appearance.

David was wearing a light khaki shirt and slacks, his sleeves rolled up, hair still very short. Coco had told me of a funny incident when they were driving round in a hired jeep. He stopped at a garage to ask the way to King's Cross (Sydney's Soho) and the guy there had slapped David on the shoulder and winked, obviously mistaking him for a young army officer with a pick-up!

When the tyre was fixed, we went to a couple of clubs. Things were still pretty quiet for us as people didn't know David was in town. He chatted to me about Japan, now only two weeks away. "You'll love it Sean!"

Fans do anything to meet their idols, but they're also terribly polite. They would climb into his hotel avoiding the security guards and the first thing he would know was the sound of feet behind him in the corridor. He'd turn and they'd stop and bow. Then he would carry on and hear them pounding along behind him again. He used to sign a few autographs and explain he was busy and they would all bow and disappear.

We ended up at the Manzil Room, a popular club in King's Cross. Tonight it was quite full but we found a table. David was in pain as he had scraped his shin getting out of the car. He pulled up the leg of his slacks to look at the damage. I applied a napkin of ice from our ice-bucket. "Shall I kiss it better?"

"You can kiss me better!"

So I did, at some length. No one took any notice.

Friday evening we flew to Adelaide, 700 miles away. It was a beautiful warm night, a clear sky full of unfamiliar stars and I tried to spot the Southern Cross constellation - till Eric grabbed my arm as I wandered across the tarmac.

Saturday was fine and sunny. We drove through town to the Oval. Adelaide was a strange city to my English eyes. The streets were wide like an American town but the buildings were European.

This was our first open-air gig, the huge rig looking magnificent with a canopy covering the stage and lights, in case of rain. We all strolled out front on the grass while support group the Angels did a sound-check. This was a great luxury after so many concrete stadiums and catacomb dressing-rooms. The back-stage area was a pleasant camp of tents and caravan trailers, potted trees to provide shade and the limos looking sleek in the sun. This tour turned out to be a refreshing holiday after the relentless pace of the US and European tours.

When the gates opened there was a good-natured stampede for the front. Back-stage David had a television in his caravan and called me across to see a new group he really liked, Dire Straits. The show included music with news and chat. They mentioned acts visiting Australia, "There's Peter Frampton and David Bowie, or on the other side, Bette Midler."

"Haven't you been watching much telly?" he asked.

"No," I said, "I never switch one on."

"Oh, you should, some of the ads are hilarious."

He told me about the macho tone - "There's one beer that has *the Mark of a Man!*" he imitated.

"What - has it got a cock as a trademark?"

"This car," cried David, "is for *Real Men* who do *Manly Things*, drink beer and throw up!"

"This caravan is for men only," added Coco, looking in at the door.

"There's this marvellous ad for Ragers Shoes," he went on. "There's a changing-room full of hearty jocks who've just played a game of rugby or something and they're all putting on these shoes. 'If you're going out *raging* tonight (David's broadest Aussie accent), you should be wearing

Ragers. And if you're not going out raging... you should be wearing *slippers*!'"

By now it was getting dark and the sound of the Angels was rolling over the crowd. It was also getting quite cold and there was a breeze.

"You ought to wrap up, David." said Coco.

"Oh, I can't do that."

"He's impossible," she said. "I've got all his woollen things packed. Oh well, I'll just have to burn his shirts with the iron!"

"NOW FOR THE FIRST TIME EVER IN AUSTRALIA..."

It may have been cold but it was one hell of a show - the first for four months, everyone a little nervous, and the glory of playing outside and to such a joyful crowd.

"We're just going off for ten minutes," announced David, half way through, "and when we come back... *we won't be wearing slippers!*"

The crowd went crazy in the second half. People were throwing streamers on-stage, also a sparkler, a camera sling and a blue muppet wearing a DEVO badge. Towards the end, Carlos was losing his voice and David forgot some of the words in 'Station To Station'. But we stormed through the encores, then down off the stage, across the grass and into the cars. The police swung the gates open and we swept back to the hotel.

We all went out that night to a posh but boring night club at the top of a high block in town but didn't stay late as we had an early start the next day.

It was a two hour flight to Perth in Western Australia. This was about 1500 miles and we flew much of the way across water, the Great Australian Bight. It was strange to think that the nearest land to our left was Antarctica!

Perth was bathed in fierce sunshine. We stayed at the gleaming modern Sheraton overlooking a wide stretch of water dotted with little sailing boats. My room had a notice saying *Welcome to the most remote capital city in the world.*

Next morning I went out with Simon and a few of the crew. We hired a tiny catamaran each. There wasn't much breeze but I drifted about happily in the sun. There were jellyfish, nearly transparent in the shallow water, and cormorants diving. A large pelican lumbered across on lazy wings just a few feet above the water. I was out there for three hours and began to feel a dangerous tingling on my back. Sure enough that night I had to sleep on my stomach and I was lucky not to have been more badly burned.

We were playing indoors in the Perth Entertainment Centre, a new circular building seating 7,500.

Notes from Perth: First show, bloke in front row, short hair, drill shirt, leather strap (camera?) looking very serious and uninvolved. Later, crowds surge forward. Two bronzed blondes in black dresses. Someone throws a sleeveless pullover on-stage. Later D picks it up and puts it on.

After the show I went out with Carlos and a few of the crew. We walked through the sleeping streets to an unlikely place called Hernando's Hideaway, above a bank. I paid a couple of dollars but Carlos refused, "You don't charge Bowie's band!" There was live music, good musicians but very untogether. Someone explained that nearly all the musicians in town had gone to our gig so this was a scratch band made up of the few who didn't like Bowie!

Next day Carlos, Roger and I found a Thai restaurant. It wasn't too fancy but the food was excellent and the service discreet but friendly, which in Eastern style means shy but with laughter.

Before the show that night a couple of pissed-up policemen tried to barge their way back-stage but Eric kept them out. They were off duty and from another state so they had no right to be there. They promised us trouble back east but this obviously never materialised.

After the show, David called to say they were going out to Connections. We were a well-guarded party - David, Coco and me, with Stu and Bob and Rick, David's Australian minders who were karate teachers. Bob had a mane of fiery red hair but was otherwise calm. Rick was blonde with the slim figure of a body-builder and rather self-consciously good-looking, to the amusement of the three of us.

Connections was a large modern disco full of people who'd seen the show - many gay. We managed to find a table and Bob and Rick stood about to prevent David being bothered.

"I wish those two weren't so obvious," muttered Stu.

We chatted over drinks and occasionally someone would come over for a few words. We discussed the merits of various guys and girls. I didn't cruise – my sunburn was too painful! Later when we trooped out, Bob and Rick mounted a rearguard action against the rush of people who suddenly decided not to be so cool as David was about to disappear from their lives. Outside a couple of kids called him over to autograph their car.

Thursday was a day off. Paul Dainty, the promoter, had hired a motor launch so a party of us went for a trip up the Swan River. It was a glorious day and most of us were in shorts or swim suits. Stu had fun trying his hand at piloting. Coco and Ron had me take their photo together – they usually don't see eye to eye.

We were talking about the shape some of us were in. I told David it was good to see him looking healthier than he used to with a tan and not so skinny. He pinched a small fold of flesh on his sparse frame and made a face.

"But I can't be flabby!" he complained. "One reviewer described me as '*nearly plump!*'"

Next day, Friday, we flew back east to Melbourne. We stayed in the Hilton overlooking the famous Melbourne Cricket Ground where we were to play tomorrow. That night I went out with Lee and Helen, a young Australian couple I had met years ago in Switzerland. We went to a slightly spit 'n' sawdust bar then on to a French restaurant which felt unbelievably civilised.

Saturday dawned distinctly grey and threatening. We went across for a wet sound-check. A light drizzle was gusting onto the stage and everything was covered in plastic sheets, looking more like a DEVO gig I guess! That night we were escorted under umbrellas from our caravan to the stage. It was pouring and the bedraggled fans had a punk look with their ruined hair and streaky make-up. But the mood was fantastic - when you're soaked you don't give a damn!

David loved the rain but the shiny black stage was like wet ice, and once he slipped and nearly went arse-over-tit into the front row! Leroy ran on to mop the stage and David wiped the soles of his shoes between numbers. Simon dried his violin bow every now and then.

In the second half, David introduced us while Dennis measured out the intro to 'Five Years'.

"Old-timer Carlos Alomar!... Living-legend Dennis Davis!..."

The crowd were going wild. One girl in shiny red pants was lifted bodily above the heads. Down the front two guys were blowing desperate kisses. One girl appeared to be crying - or was it the rain? During the encores, a few fireworks went off and one or two rockets soared up onto the canopy. For a moment I wondered if the plastic was fireproof... then realised it hardly mattered!

Lee and Helen joined me just as I finished showering. We chatted over a couple of beers then the phone rang. It was David, "Quick - Quentin Crisp's on TV!"

Next morning it was still wet when we drove out to the airport. The driver was very cheerful and sent a puddle of water all over a motorcyclist. Two minutes later we saw a woman pushing a car off the road on the other side.

"Hey, that's my wife!" cried our driver. "I'll be back soon," he shouted to her and we continued to the airport.

We were shown to a private departure room. There was a giant silver Christmas tree and paper bells. It was Sunday, 19th November. We chatted for a while until Ron told us it was time to move. As we took off, the rain on the windows was blown back in streaks and we surfaced through the clouds into bright sunshine. Down below the dried-out, dusty river beds were now full of muddy water. The air hostesses were friendly and Dennis was soon walking one of them up the aisle introducing us all.

"He plays tuba," he said, pointing to Tony Mascia. Simon and I became roadies. Then a bouncing baby appeared above a seat... "and that's David!"

Brisbane is the capital of Queensland, the vast state forming the north-east of Australia and known in Sydney as the Deep North. The weather was warm but wet. We booked into the hotel early in the afternoon and had a late lunch. The food was truly dreadful, tough and tasteless steaks. David looked embarrassed when the manager asked how he found the meal.

"It's very... um... interesting," he reported.

Monday (November 20th) was a beautiful, hot sunny day so Carlos and I hired bicycles and spent a glorious afternoon in a park with palm trees, lizards and tropical flowers. Later, we wandered into town where the big stores were trimming up for Christmas.

Early evening I wrote to Penny.

Tour's great, lots of free time in the sun.

But whoever heard of a tanned punk? Haven't seen the Southern Cross or a kangaroo yet but David is looking divine as his crew cut grows out.

I had a solitary dinner in the hotel then Pat, Coco, Rick and David appeared back from a Japanese restaurant. David, a little drunk, put his arm round me and asked what was happening. We were in the lobby and flicked through the book-stand. I saw a magazine called *Young Australians* and suggested it as a song title. David saw a book by Herman Hesse and decided to pinch it, stuffing it down his baggy Chinese pants. Pat and Rick were outside. David wanted to take a jeep but Pat forbade him to drive. While they were all talking, David crept away and ran for the jeep like a truant schoolboy. I followed him, everyone piled in and we headed for the club.

We went up to the 30th floor by express elevator. David and I were last and the manager came over and stopped us. I was in my leather jacket and David wore a light V-neck pullover, no shirt. We backed off, laughing, and Pat whispered in the guy's embarrassed ear.

Inside everyone was already celebrating at a long table - it was Tony's first wedding anniversary and the champagne was flowing freely. Dennis was playing drums with the group - all girls. David and Leroy had a dance - they did the Bump then Leroy picked him up and they both fell over a chair taking a guest with them. Later on, I saw David leave the dance-floor arm-in-arm with a girl, then her boyfriend rushed up and took her other arm. David let her go, laughing.

After Coco and I left, they all went on to another club with a revolving floor.

"It was great," David told me, "you could start chatting up one girl and end up with another!"

Next day we drove out to Lang Park for the gig. Fans were literally camping at the gates with canvas awnings spread above sleeping-bags.

The show that night was great fun. The crowd were very lively as often happens in a repressive area. One girl down the front kept fainting and being lifted out of the crowd over the barrier to recover. I just wondered if she was faking it.

After the gig, we went for something to eat and had a funny meal, everyone in a silly mood. David put on my leather jacket and clowned about. We ended up throwing paper darts around the place. David loaded the nose of one with a small coin and it disappeared down the stairs.

David (to Rob): "Did you see the girl who was hauled over the front of the stage several times?"

Rob: "Yes."

David: "Interested?"

Rob (enthusiastic): "Yes!"

David: "I met *him* later at that club!"

Next morning I looked through the paper to see how they liked us. There were several articles, all about the nuisance value of the concert: "OPEN-AIR POP? MORE OF A SMELLY MELÉE" – this headed 500 words devoted to armpits and the physical discomfort of standing in a crowd of 10,000. Another, about noise, was headed "SOME GLUM OVER DAVID'S STRUM." On the front page was a short piece headed "Noisy Feedback... Pop singer David Bowie got some noisy feedback from the minister in charge of noise abatement, Mr. Russ Hinze: 'These pop singers come out here to make a quick quid by disturbing our peace and tranquillity,' Mr. Hinze said. 'The fact that he's a Pommie as well wouldn't help.'" (I believe Mr. Hinze became Prime Minister of Queensland – it must be wonderfully quiet there...)

So the Pommie and his band flew back to Sydney and the Sebel Town House. That evening, Coco and I walked through a pleasant back street to the Manzil Room. There was a band playing and the place was pretty full. Our crowd was there as well as some of Bette Midler's band, who jammed on-stage with Dennis and Roger.

Leroy grabbed me and introduced three punk girls, Trina, Linda and Maggie. They had seen the show in

Adelaide and were delighted to see a punk on-stage. They shared a flat at the other end of Kings Cross so later we went back there. Trina was all in black, a shiny sleeveless top and tight vinyl shorts, net tights and stiletto heels, with black gloves and white-frame dark glasses. It was wolf whistles all the way through Kings Cross, with the girls standing in doorways.

Back at the flat we drank, smoked, talked until 6am, about people, clothes, music, here and elsewhere, and not at all about David Bowie.

Next day I met Coco again at the hotel.

"How were the punkettes?"

"Oh fine, I've just got myself a girlfriend."

She and David were going to see Bette's show that night and suggested I come along. So that evening I took the lift to the top of the hotel and padded along the thick carpeted corridor to the Presidential Suite. The TV was on softly, the screen pink. I don't know if David had been playing with the knobs. He told me he had been over to see Peter Frampton at his hotel.

"He's very friendly, just as sweet as he used to be at school!"

Then he put on his crumpled suit and we were ready to go.

The State Theatre was a richly decorated old building with statues, chandeliers and marble floors. We were ushered into the packed theatre, standing at the back as the show was a sell-out. It was a marvellous, hilarious and dazzling show. I was amazed how Bette had managed to get familiar with all the local jokes and put-downs, ramming home her gleefully bitchy asides.

Our first Sydney show seemed subdued though it went well. When I got back to the hotel Trina, Linda and Maggie came round with a multicoloured punk cake for Linda's birthday. We went downstairs to see if anyone else fancied joining the party.

I was surprised to see David in the lobby among a crowd of avid fans. Trina called out to him – "Want some birthday cake?"

"Well, hi there!" he said. "How are you?"

"I'm fine," replied Trina. "How are you?"

"I'm wonderful!"

"Get you!" screamed Maggie.

Saturday, Trina and I woke late. We went round to the flat for Maggie to dye and cut my hair. She didn't bother with gloves so her hands came out navy blue. They were shaking too as she wielded the scissors – she had put away most of the Chivas Regal last night!

The show that night was our last in Australia and it was a stunner, one of the best of the whole tour. Everyone was electrified – eight of us on-stage and 12,000 out there. I soon spotted the three punkettes at the front.

Simon was dressed all in black with a white scarf hanging down. During his solo in 'Jean Genie', he was silhouetted in the spotlight, the wind blowing his hair and scarf, looking like the demon fiddler.

"The wind always seems to blow in my solos!" he said later.

'Breaking Glass' - *I never touch you... No, no, no (echo) I can't find you... I can't see you... I can't hear you* (great cheer) *My, my! a-whoa-whoa, My, My!*

The second half was a romp. We came off after 'Station To Station' and Coco handed David his sailor cap. He put it on backwards and we ran out again.

Oh my TVC15... oh-oh!

For the second encore, David returned alone. He stood there leaning on the mike stand, the spotlights holding him while the rapturous noise broke over him like heavy surf.

What would you do if I sang out of tune - would you stand up and walk out on me? NO!!!

Then he started everyone singing along to a beer commercial - *Have another Tooey, have another Tooey, have another Tooey or two!*

"We'll be back next year - I promise!"

As we drove across town in the fleet of white limos a few car-loads of kids tagged along. When we stopped at traffic lights a smart young couple were walking by and the girl peered at us.

"No! It's him? I don't believe it!"

Sunday was our last day in Australia. That afternoon we drove out of town and relaxed at Dennis Garcia's place, a bungalow near a small lake. Trina and I got a lift back with a strange bunch of country boys in an old banger. They stopped on the way at a deserted house where they used to live. It was eerie. Then it was back over the Harbour Bridge.

Monday morning I packed and had breakfast with Trina and a girlfriend, causing quite a stir in the staid restaurant with their bright pink and green tights. Then it was goodbye, off to the airport and we were soon winging our way to New Zealand.

CHAPTER 16

NEW ZEALAND

Monday, 27th November

Christchurch must be one of quietest cities in the world. Noah's Hotel was pleasant enough and overlooked a small river with green banks, willow trees and little bridges, which reminded me of Cambridge. The first night we played pinball in the hotel till 5am. The next night we went to some bad movies including a documentary about a petrol economy race. Now, even in 1978 I was ecologically aware, but if you're after the 'Oscar for Deadly Movie of the Year', you couldn't do better than a petrol economy race. There was also a punk movie which must have been made by right-wing elements aiming to put people off punk. So it was back to pinball at Noah's.

Wednesday was the gig. It was open-air and went well

enough. The back-stage area was surrounded by a bamboo fence and security was in the capable hands of large Maoris. The tour programme listed 'Lizzy Stardust' - *Lizzy played guitar...*! That night we finally got to a club. It was very subdued and formal. We had to sit at a table. No one was allowed to approach the bar or walk about holding a drink. I soon gave up and went back to bed.

Thursday night we were still there. Coco rang. "Hullo, guess what we've got up here - Thai food! Want to come up?"

"I found out one of the chefs here is from Thailand," David explained as I tucked in eagerly, "and he offered to cook some Thai dishes specially, they're not on the menu. He's really done us proud, there's far more than we can eat."

Our conversation was animated, ranging from World War II to a television interview David had done a couple of nights ago. The popular chat-show compere was smugly trying to lead David and even suggested that his 'bisexuality' was a fraudulent publicity stunt - homosexuality was completely illegal in New Zealand at this time.

"Of course," said the man, "you're not claiming to be bisexual nowadays, are you?"

"Yes," David replied simply, "I am bisexual, that was a genuine statement."

I finally admitted defeat on the food and we left the table a gleaming battleground of dishes. We listened to Dire Straits and Hawkwind, Simon's former group.

"I haven't listened to anything by them for ages," he said, "but I really like this. Simon gave me a cassette."

Later David asked me what was happening in Christchurch. I told him, "Really the only lively place in town is the pinball room downstairs!"

"Oh splendid!" cried David and we all went down and joined the crowd round the machines.

Next day we flew north. From the air the scenery was beautiful - green thickly-wooded mountains and blue sea. I was sorry I hadn't hired a car and got out of town.

We passed around a slide viewer with Roger's slides. At home he had linked his synthesizers to a computer monitor and the music generated colour graphics. David was fascinated and had fun putting two slides in at once, giving a 3-D effect.

"I can never leave sources alone!" he commented.

Auckland on North Island is a much bigger, livelier place. We swept through the city and over a huge bridge, finally nosing down little roads of holiday bungalows to our hotel. The Mon Desir was a single-storey complex, the full length windows of each room sliding open onto the garden, beyond which lay the beach.

But I was soon off to the VD clinic, returning with a bottle of pills and a notice that sexual intercourse while infected could render you liable to imprisonment. Even in those carefree days, a minor infection was taken seriously. Oh well, no sex for a week.

I wandered over to the restaurant and had dinner with Rick, David's blond Australian bodyguard, and he told me about covering the Fleetwood Mac tour in Japan. David and Coco joined us, "Just for drinks," said David, but Rick also had some brandy snaps.

The restaurant was quite full by now, mostly young people and a few autograph hunters among them. Someone sent a note via the waiter offering to do David's hair, joking, "or would skydiving be possible?" David wrote back that Rick was his private hairdresser.

Coco asked me about clubs in town. "You've been here three hours."

"Yes," I said, "but I spent two of them at the hospital."

We were soon into a lively discussion of tropical poxes, "a favourite topic of Jim's," said David, and a calculation of how many 'free' days I would get in Japan. The conversation moved via crabs to creepy-crawlies and Coco described finding a nest of adders under her bed in Albuquerque while filming *The Man Who Fell To Earth*. David had set up a studio there so he could paint while not filming, and snakes had got into everything.

"Iggy loves reptiles. That's where his name comes from - iguana!"

We talked about fans and fan mail. Coco told me about a man up north who worked out a whole social system derived from David's songs.

"I've sometimes thought of putting a book together. And

all the artists – I used to encourage them back in the fan club days to organise exhibitions."

Later, David told me about security at the airport here.

"There was a double-phalanx of big guys in black uniforms, but no crowds, just five photographers!"

Coco described one encounter in Tokyo when David was on a private visit. There were just the three of them, David, Coco and Iggy, no security – and five thousand Japanese fans! David was rescued by a big guard who picked him up and carried him bodily over the heads of the crowd. By way of contrast, I told them about Fumble's encounter with two fans in Glasgow back in '73. I'm glad to say David was amused.

We went through to the bar which was busy and I got beers for them and a coke for myself. David said quietly, "What do you think all these people do for a living?"

I looked around.

"I bet you anything you like," he said, "they're all hair-dressers!"

I laughed – he had to be right!

A couple of the band joined us briefly, one of them lamenting an enforced state of celibacy.

"Perhaps I'm aiming too high," he complained. "I think I'll start a Principle of Intercontinental Happiness – ICH – for getting into ugly women."

"Stu has beaten you to it," David laughed.

Then Dennis appeared in an immaculate white suit and came over to us quietly.

"I'm Fred Johnson, the manager," he announced politely. "Is everything all right. Mr. B? Mr. Mayes?... Yes? Well, far fucking out." He turned to the nearest hairdressers. "I hope everything is fine? If not," he added, turning back to us confidentially, "well, fuck you." He sat down beside David and continued, "I've got this ranch on 125th and 7th Avenue..."

We both shouted with laughter and some of the hairdressers shifted nervously. Up till then they had only dared occasional discreet glances.

Eric joined us, in a very cheerful mood. He was well pleased with the hotel. The promoter had tried to put us in another place where he was staying with the rest of the tour party but Eric had resisted.

"He rang me up just now," he told us gleefully, "and said the fire extinguishers had gone off and flooded all their rooms!"

Coco went off to bed and David went to the loo while Rick and I were chatting. He seemed to be gone rather a long time so I said something to Rick and he went off like a shot. He came back with David a minute later.

"There was a looney in the loo," David explained. "He kept talking to me and I didn't know how to get away without being rude. I don't know what it is, they always seem to pick on me."

"It's getting a bit bad when you have to take a bodyguard to the loo," I said. "Still I suppose you're bound to attract some attention."

"Oh, but I don't think he recognised me. I've just always been one of those people drunks talk to."

Sober but content, I fell asleep that night watching fairy lights on the trees outside through my hessian net curtain.

Next day, Saturday, was the gig, but in the morning David took a jeep out with Coco, Rick and me to go walking over the cliffs. On the way back we passed a camp site and saw the distinctive red clothes and white beard of Father Christmas entertaining a crowd of kids in the hot midday sun.

As we drove out to the gig early that evening there was a strong sense of anticipation. It was almost like a Hitchcock movie - the monotonous flat bungalowed suburbs seemingly deserted, but every street an endless line of parked cars. Somewhere above droned a helicopter, and the car radio was telling people there was no more parking space for a couple of miles in any direction.

I was with Pat and Eric who were discussing the possibility of breaking the New Zealand crowd record. As we got closer, we saw people on foot in greater numbers and the limo hooted gently to clear a path. Some of the kids crowded around the car, very excited, and I had a moment of panic, a taste of what it's like to be threatened by the desire of a thousand people to rush up and touch. Then we reached the haven of safety, the back-stage camp.

Western Springs is a huge open-air stadium, one side a natural amphitheatre. Every now and then we heard a new report about the size of the crowd. It had passed 25,000 quite early on and grew to thirty, then thirty-five. Finally it reached 41,000 – the largest crowd ever in New Zealand, beating the early record of the Stones and even Neil Diamond!

The first half went well, though the place was so big that we lost much of the immediacy of the audience. When we went on for the second half, David suggested we all take our cameras and photograph the crowd. He never carries a camera nowadays (he had a small Polaroid in 1973) but borrowed Roger's so he could join us in this 'tribute' to our audience. At the end of the show, he flung his sailor cap out to them as we ran off for the last time.

Sunday 3rd December, was our last day in the Southern Hemisphere, our last day of summer. I went for a swim in the sea to celebrate. Then we packed up and drove out to the airport. We flew out from Auckland at 7.30pm, arriving in Sydney four hours later. I posted a letter to Trina. Then we embarked on a small jet bound for Tokyo.

CHAPTER 17

JAPAN

Monday, 4th December

To step onto the plane was to step into Japan. The hostesses wore kimonos and their courtesy seemed traditional. The cover of the flight magazine showed a Japanese shrub with red berries and dark green leaves dusted with snow. I gave a deep sigh as if I was achieving some goal and felt deeply excited to be speeding towards a country more different than any I had ever seen.

We touched down on the dark tarmac at 6.00am. Tokyo New International Airport at Narita was very cold, mostly dull grey concrete, neon-lit. Customs waved me through but went through Carlos's bags very carefully.

Out on the concourse we were greeted by Mr. Udo, the tour promoter, a genial, dapper man, while a TV crew filmed our arrival and journalists descended for interviews. David had already gone through and disappeared.

The cold light of dawn was competing with a matrix of neon tubes high above our heads like our stage rig. A poster caught my eye – the head of a fierce warrior pointing two fingers at his nose. The only English caption said Hitachi Gallery but we decided it was an ad for tranquillisers – *When problems are getting up your nose...*

We drove through heavily guarded barriers into three hours of the worst traffic jams I have ever seen, and the forty mile run took nearly as long as our flight from Australia. We dozed sweatily in the rising sun. When we reached it, Tokyo looked very much like any other big city but our impression was somehow different.

The Tokyo Prince Hotel, Shiba Park, Minato-ku, was large and genteel, its style combining '30s grandiose solidity with western elegance. The tour schedule warned us to behave with decorum – no T-shirts in lobby please. My room was large and luxurious with a generous bouquet of pink roses and a small card, *Dear Sean, Welcome to Japan! S. Udo.*

I joined Carlos and Dennis for a beer. This gave us an appetite and we had our first Japanese meal – *tempura* – large prawns and sliced vegetables fried in a light batter, very crisp and fresh. We toasted our arrival with hot *saké*, a colourless spirit like vodka served in little earthenware 'eggcups'.

Several of the band's wives and girlfriends flew out to join us for this last leg of the tour. Roger and Jane, his English girlfriend, were taking a taxi into town to look for bargains in camera shops so I went along. Later I returned to the hotel alone on the underground, feeling rather proud of myself, though it was only three stops on one line! I slept for a few hours then several of us spent the evening in the hotel bar, too exhausted to be more enterprising.

Next morning we caught the bullet train - *Hikari* - to Osaka. When this train first ran it was the fastest in the world, reaching 150mph. The carriages are long and slim and the engine has a bullet-shaped nose. I enjoyed the journey and found it rather tantalising to watch the countryside flash past so quickly - pretty patchworks of small fields and peasants in traditional clothes working with wooden tools. A couple of schoolkids in bright baseball caps looked up as we passed. It was so picturesque I suspected the Japanese Tourist Board of staging it. But we barely glimpsed the familiar cone of Mount Fujii, obscured by clouds and telegraph wires.

Wednesday, 6th December

Japan is a string of islands of the same area and climate as Britain. Osaka is a huge industrial city to the south and we were to play two gigs here and two in Tokyo. We stayed in a large modern hotel with oriental touches like a roof garden of (Zen-style?) combed gravel.

I strolled to the station and found a cheap restaurant for a late breakfast of *sushi* - little blocks of rice with raw fish - hot soup and brown tea. I gave my order by pointing to plastic models displayed in the window. During the three hours I was away from the hotel I saw not one Western face and met no one who spoke a word of English but I managed to buy a pair of gloves, a lens cleaner, some hair conditioner, sticking-plaster and a pictorial map of Japan. By then I was lost. Only the largest streets in a Japanese city have names, signposts are written in Japanese and anyway I didn't know what to ask for! But at last I found the station and got my bearings again.

It was a cheerful gathering at the theatre with most of the band's wives and girlfriends there. I also met Anthony, a mannered but genial Englishman living in Kyoto who was doing David's subtle stage make-up.

From 41,000 in New Zealand we now faced a capacity crowd of 1500 in the small Kosei Nenkin Theatre. The audience was polite and enthusiastic but there was no hysteria. One kid had died at a big concert earlier this year when the crowd rushed the stage, so now they were strictly controlled.

The music was enlivened by Dennis who had two huge Chinese gongs behind him which he struck whenever the mood took him. As he gradually became more enthusiastic these were confiscated! After the show, Ishi, a young man looking after us for the promoter, Mr. Udo, took us to a small disco. We paid 2000 yen admission, then drinks – Japanese beer and whisky – were free. The place was dull and I didn't stay long.

Next day everyone had hangovers when we gathered in the coffee-shop. I made a list of people to send postcards - it came to over 100 so I wrote *Merry Christmas* on them to save myself the trouble when I got home.

The show that night was livelier - people threw streamers and there seemed to be quite a few gays. Dennis decorated his face with Red Indian-style warpaint. The crowd were certainly more responsive and there was even applause for the start of 'Sense Of Doubt'! David spoke a few words of Japanese which produced a noisy response.

That night a small party of us went to dinner with Mr. Yamamoto, the head of RCA in Japan. The restaurant speciality was Kobe beef which is out of this world - to ensure the meat is tender they even massage the bulls!

We walked back through a covered shopping area and came upon an extraordinary Christmas display - a white plastic fir-tree stood beside a patch of artificial turf and on this stood three life-sized woolly sheep surrounded by real roses. I knelt down and aimed my pocket camera while Anthony grazed on the roses and David struck a dramatic pose embracing a sheep.

In the car, the radio played a track from the recent *Sgt. Pepper* film with the Bee Gees and Peter Frampton. I said it was funny how their shrill voices were similar to David's early accent.

"Yes," he laughed, "they'll be doing Ziggy next!"

Friday was free and most of the band were lured away to

visit the Roland instrument factory but a party of us took a trip to Kyoto, a beautiful ancient city of temples and shrines. (David had been invited to visit the old Imperial Palace which is not open to the public.) I won't attempt a travelogue account of the temples, but I took these photos of humdrum but characteristic scenes: A man with a white cloth tied around his head carries a stick over his shoulder with a knotted plastic sheet full of plants. High above the street, workmen painting a bridge look like soldiers in their khaki jackets and helmets. An old woman in clogs sits slumped on a bench with a hand to her head. A towering pylon stands in the muddy waters of a wide river, and beside it is a small fishing boat with two immobile figures.

That evening in the bar, I met a couple of fans, Jimi and Michelle (they use Western names with foreigners). I asked them if we could see any live music and we ended up in a dancehall with a Philippino group. They played assorted pop music in various languages, very sleek and fascinating but not what I had in mind. On the dance floor were twenty youths all dancing a formation exercise – a cross between *Saturday Night Fever* and *Come Dancing* performed with the concentration of a martial arts *kata*. I had a couple of drinks but decided not to join in!

Next day, Saturday, Jimi and Michelle met me for a breakfast of fish, rice and soup, then looked around the shops.

Tonight we were playing at the larger Expo Hall. It was a lively show with more streamers thrown. David caught one and mimed a tug of war with the kid at the other end. After the show, Jimi took me to a crowded bar with faces I recognised from the front row of the show. Fortunately the barman had been a sailor and was able to translate for us.

Next morning it was a scramble to catch the train. We were seen off by a small group of girls, one of them crying a lot. Three hours later as we rolled into Tokyo, I spotted a driving-school on the flat roof of a building – ten white cars nosing their way around pavements, traffic islands and even a miniature flyover – it looked like a toy shop display!

CHAPTER 18

TOKYO

This time we stayed in the New Otani Hotel, a 2000 room edifice of two three-sided tower blocks, one topped with a revolving restaurant. The hotel had twenty-seven bars and restaurants, but a coffee (with service) cost more than a cheap meal in one of the nearby streets.

My room was on the 28th floor of the taller tower. The tinted glass and rounded corners made the sealed window seem like a huge TV screen. Far below I could just make out a garden, irregular stepping stones crossing a stream.

That night I was accosted by a couple of fans, so I asked them if they knew of any punk clubs in Tokyo. They came up to my room for a drink and phoned around. They both spoke English, Yukari only a little, but Sa (pronounced Say) had spent some months in America and spoke with assurance.

As we were leaving they told me they were going to call on Keith Jarret – had I heard of him? Keith Jarret is, roughly speaking, a jazz pianist (world class).

We dropped a few floors silently in the high-speed elevator and walked the soft corridor to his room. He answered the door and invited us in. We sat on the bed and the girls introduced me and asked a few questions. Keith was polite and soft-spoken, but it slowly dawned on me that the girls had never met him before and must simply have asked for his room number at the desk. I was embarrassed and wondered how to apologise, but he was friendly and may even have been amused at the situation. I suggested he might get in touch if he'd like to meet the rest of the band, but he never did.

Then we left Mr. Jarret in peace and headed for Ropongi, Tokyo's night-life area, but the clubs were smart and dull and expensive. Back at the hotel there was a message for me to call Barbara, David's American PR.

"Sean, can you do me a big favour? There's a party after the show on Tuesday (the last night) and some of the English crowd out here are putting on a cabaret. The trouble is, they need a pianist for one song and they can't find anyone."

"What's the song – do I know it?"

"It's 'Just A Gigolo' – that's the theme of the party – you know, with David's film coming out soon."

Well, of course I agreed, wondering how on earth I would make out at '30s style piano, something new to me. So next morning found me at RCA with a piano, a cassette of a scratchy '78, and a beautiful but nervous English model who had never sung in her life before.

"I want to half-talk, half-sing my way through it in the style of Marlene Dietrich," she confided.

The session went awkwardly, both of us out of our depth. Barbara waved aside any problems. "You'll be marvellous! But not a word to anyone, especially David – it's all a surprise." A shock is how I'd have described it.

By the way, in the elevator at RCA was an intriguing sign – a notice in Japanese with little diagrams and red circles showing one building in flames and another bending and jumping. I asked what this meant. "It says, 'You must not use the elevator in case of fire or earthquake...'"

My diary says, *Show in big judo hall* – it was Budokan of course. This famous arena is the world's judo mecca, the national stadium of this martial art and sport. It is a modern structure but with traditional styling, the roof flicking up at all eight corners. Inside, over our lighting gantry hung a huge Japanese flag, the red ball of the rising sun on a white background. Eric was very excited to be there as he practices judo. In fact, I think he would have preferred the night's show to be a judo display!

Back-stage we looked at the official Japanese tour programme. This was a large glossy magazine with excellent photos, some from this tour, some from the past. The band was listed, but we were sorry that no picture of the band had been included in any of the programmes.

This show went very well and the crowd was more responsive than in Osaka, though there was still a feeling of restraint.

When I had showered and changed, I took a taxi to Vanessa's place for rehearsals for tomorrow's party. It's strange taking a taxi in Tokyo because very few of the streets have names. There's a postal system only understood by postmen – I believe the telegraph poles are numbered – but otherwise an address takes the form of the nearest big street, then 'third on the right behind the cinema' or whatever! This can make things interesting for a foreigner trying to explain to a cab driver, but Vanessa had written out instructions in Japanese, so he was able to take me to the right street, where a police-man directed me to her block.

When I walked in, Vanessa, Barbara and a friend, Maxine, were sitting around laughing while a striking model, Jeannie, went through a dance with Anthony. The record was Deitrich's 'Honeysuckle Rose' and the dance was a very sexy torch number, Jeannie trying to thaw a bored gigolo with every kind of approach. I was hardly in at the door before I was recruited to stand in for a second absent dance partner.

"Two Jap boys should be along later, so Anthony's helping out. You don't have to do much – just hold a leg now and then, and look bored."

Of course the 'boys' never showed and my look of boredom was so devastating that I was booked for the performance...

Tuesday, 12th December

This was the final night of the world tour. NHK Hall was the largest of our gigs in Japan and the show was being filmed for television. Our sound-check and run-through lasted most of the afternoon. During breaks, I silently practiced my *Gigolo* part, running my fingers lightly over the keys. No one must hear, David mustn't suspect!

Back-stage everyone seemed down – only Dennis cheered us up, pulling on an ape-head mask. Then he hid it till he was on-stage so he could give David a surprise when he turned round.

So we went on and the show began. With each BOOM! of 'Warsawa' I felt more down, and it seemed everyone else felt that way too. With each song we played I just thought, "I'll never play this again."

Next was 'What In The World', then 'Be My Wife'. Then we came to 'Jean Genie' and something was triggered, the adrenalin flooded through me – *I'm in Tokyo on-stage with David Bowie playing 'Jean Genie', here and now, once and for all!* This spark seemed to flash through the whole group, and from that moment the show took off and became a stormer, one of the best of the whole tour, all the higher for starting low.

Jean Genie – let yourself go!

In the limo going back to the hotel, I was already spitting on tissues to clean off my make-up. I ran through the lobby, had the fastest shower and got to the Bee Club by 9.45pm.

We went through the numbers and they worked. A lady violinist was added for *Gigolo,* the perfect touch – we made a mournful sound like an old tea room duo.

In honour of David Bowie you are cordially invited to a 'gigolo party' on December 12th, 1978 at 10.30pm.

Dress: 1920's style optional, black tie.

By 11pm the place was packed. I don't suppose a single invitation was declined. It was difficult clearing a space on the dance floor for our cabaret, and then impossible to liaise with the disc jockey. When at last we heard the strains of 'Honeysuckle Rose', it sounded as if Marlene was on a long-distance phone call. Suddenly she blasted out at full volume and we coolly performed the dance. No one dropped anyone and it went well. As the number ended, I slid onto the piano stool, and with a rustle of silk the violinist launched into 'Just a Gigolo'. Vanessa stood at my shoulder and chanted the words in husky, world weary tones. The cabaret ended with a hilarious tango from Anthony and Maxine, who performed with a stuffed raven perched on her gloved fingers.

Then the crowd took possession of the dance floor again. I swapped my white shirt and dinner jacket for stripes and leather (still wearing the black tie).

David was the centre of attention of course, and I only saw him briefly. He had enjoyed the show and Coco was amused because David had failed to recognise me until halfway through the dance number.

It was a good party. The guests were mostly European and Americans living in Tokyo, with a sprinkling of Japanese. The fancy/formal dress gave the club a sparkling style, like bubbles in the free champagne. The stage-crew were there, some of them in suits which must have been packed for the whole tour. I went around saying farewells, and gave Carlos a big goodbye kiss that had Robin raising her eyebrows!

I noticed a striking Japanese punk couple who might have been brother and sister.

"Hello," I said, "I don't know who you are, but I'd love to meet you."

Toshi and Chica (who were not brother and sister) are a couple of designers and also have a punk group, Plastics. We struck up an immediate friendship and they invited me round to their studio, giving me an unusual card with the address.

Gradually the guests thinned out. Tomorrow, most of the group were flying out to spend Christmas at home or somewhere in the sun. I had decided to stay on for a week and see more of Tokyo. As the final stragglers departed, Simon and I were bashing out rock 'n' roll on the piano.

★ ★ ★

That night at the party I met a girl with whom I had a brief affair. On Wednesday night, the two of us went to a few clubs and in one they were playing a Bing Crosby Christmas album. Competing with this was the noise from two or three electronic pinball machines, coming at us from different directions. The combined effect was like a bizarre new-wave Christmas record.

On Thursday, we went shopping in Harajuku, a broad modern boulevard with some fascinating stores. I didn't make it to the Ginza, which is more famous, but I believe it's very expensive and only worth window-shopping. In Harajuku there is a fascinating toyshop, Kiddyland, with many magical floors of toys and games which soon had me as excited as any child. I bought an armful of presents for my friends' kids, and also a few I couldn't resist myself!

Another fascinating place was the Oriental Bazaar. It looked like a mixture of museum and market, but all for sale. Everything I saw brought to mind a friend who would love it, and I was soon laden with presents, lacquer, silk, chopsticks and cigarette lighters.

My 'girlfriend' took care of these for me and I went off to look for Toshi and Chica's studio, which was not far away.

I left the main street, spotted a small post office and went in hopefully. No one spoke English but they passed my card around cheerfully, then one of the girls came from behind the counter and signed for me to follow her. We crossed the road and plunged into narrow winding back streets. After a few minutes an old man appeared, wavering slowly towards us on a bicycle. She spoke to him, then politely left me in his care. He took me further into the area until we spotted a young fellow on a moped delivering newspapers. He left his bike running and led me down back alleys till at last we came to a small block of flats. He insisted on taking me right up to the door, and didn't leave until we were sure I had the right place.

Toshi and Chica were not at the studio, but a friend made me welcome, though she spoke no English. She phoned them, and we arranged to meet later that night.

On my way out of the labyrinth I was surprised to come upon a punk clothes shop. I looked in and talked to the people running it, but all the goods were British. I would have loved some Japanese punk clothes.

I got back to the hotel, wondering if I would see David again. Then Coco rang to invite me to dinner. We met in George's room. His wife Jennifer was here and we all went out to a small restaurant, off the beaten track where few Westerners go. It was a fascinating experience.

The first thing which struck me as the door opened was the din. The barrage of voices was the loudest I had ever heard in any restaurant in my life. There was scarcely any room to enter as the place was nearly filled by a large bar. Around three sides of this, the diners sat on stools. Behind the bar the floor was raised, and two chefs knelt on cushions cooking food which they selected from a crowded array in front of them. They passed small dishes out to the diners on long wooden spatulas, also serving them with cold beer and hot *saké* in this way.

We were soon perched on high stools against the bar. Waiters circulated in the narrow space behind the diners, taking our orders then shouting these to the chefs with much humour and back chat. Since every meal consisted of at least a dozen dishes and the waiters called for each item as it was needed, the low room reverberated with staccato sing-song shouting, and the chefs joined in the cheerful banter.

The waiters were dressed in rough blue skirted overalls and oriental clogs as the floor was slippery. The two chefs wore headbands to control the sweat and worked more quickly and deftly than I have ever seen. Behind them was a bright shrine displaying wooden prayer tablets, flowers, pictures, paper fans and other religious (*Shinto*) bric-a-brac. It was obvious that, for all the clamour, the restaurant was devoted to the art of good eating. The food was delicious, but extremely varied and occasionally disconcerting. I managed to crunch the tiny glazed whole crabs David offered me. Some dishes remained a mystery.

The evening was also delightful as David was in the company of a charming Japanese girl who entertained us with an informal Japanese lesson, showing how words are formed by simple pictures, and helping us to write our names in Japanese.

After the meal, I left and got a taxi to NHK Hall, which now loomed dark and brooding in the empty car park, so different from the show on Tuesday night. Toshi was waiting for me there and we walked a short distance to their flat. This was small and chaotic, full of books, records, papers, much like my own place!

They had a friend with them who also spoke English, and I think they regarded him as a kind of guru. Talk ranged over music, politics, fashions, ideas, youth, age and the world today. They told me how punk fashion had caught on with Japanese kids, but not the music, although some of the more commercial new-wave bands were successful, of course.

They described a few gigs they had managed to stage, which were something like dadaist 'happenings'. They were fascinated and horrified at the influence of the worst aspects of western commercialism on Japanese life, and how so few people, young or old, have any ideas of their own.

Toshi was a graphic designer and Chica worked in fashion and photography – sometimes they collaborated on projects. We talked until late, then they drove me back to the hotel, my head ringing with ideas.

Friday, 15th December

I went to see David and Coco next morning. They were staying at a traditional Japanese hotel. It was very quiet and dignified, and they would probably behead any teeny-bop fan who dared to put a nose inside the door. I felt like an intruder in my leather jacket – still at least my hair looked Japanese! I went up to their suite.

Coco let me in. I removed my boots just inside the door

before stepping onto the low platform of rush matting which formed the floor. The room was quite small and unpretentious, in muted colours, with a minimum of furniture. I did not attempt an eastern pose, but tried to sprawl elegantly while drinking brown tea.

We drove right across Tokyo to Asakusa, an old part of the city where the Sensu-ji Temple of Kannon presides over a cheerful bazaar. We wandered around the colourful shops and had a meal in a small restaurant, then walked through to the temple. At the entrance were two fierce, red, muscular gods with swirling sashes who guard the temple, themselves protected by wire netting. Behind the gateway above our heads was a pair of giant sandals - in case the god Kannon should wake and wish to come forth. Apparently he lives in a holy sanctum at the centre of the temple, and this is sealed, so not even the priests may enter.

It was getting dark and the bazaar was alive with lights. There was some activity around the temple and workmen in helmets (or were they priests?) were erecting large banners with the help of long wooden ladders. A group of girls approached us diffidently - David had been spotted. He spoke with them and signed a couple of autographs, then explained that he was now on holiday and needed to relax, and at his request they politely withdrew. There was a pleasant tang of woody incense on the evening air as we walked back to the car.

Saturday, 16th December

I went to see Pat and sorted out the balance of my money, ending up with fistfulls of yen. I was leaving on Monday, so today was probably my last chance to buy any presents. I went out and bought some Japanese pop magazines near the hotel, and bumped into Sa (whom I met during my first evening back in Tokyo). We exchanged addresses and the following summer she came to stay with me in London, where in the course of two months she managed to see a total of 45 groups!

Then I took the underground for a last visit to Kiddyland and the Oriental Bazaar, emerging in the busy streets at Shinjuku... and realised I had blundered. I had got the wrong station, and hadn't a clue about the right one.

What could I do? I phoned the hotel and reached someone who spoke English. She told me I wanted Harajuku. My tube map showed I was on the wrong line, but there was an overground line linking the stations so I might make it. The mainline station was seething with rush hour commuters - long queues at dozens of ticket-windows and everything written in Japanese. No one spoke English, but in my second queue I finally got a ticket and the platform number, wading through the crowds to find the train. *Harajuku?* Yes!

As we pulled out, a couple of students started talking to me in broken English. Five minutes later I nearly missed my stop, but squeezed through the doors with just enough time to sprint down the road to the shops.

Later I returned to David's hotel, where Coco was up to her eyes in packing and last minute arrangements. She and David were spending Christmas in Kyoto with Anthony. We exchanged small presents and kissed goodbye. In the taxi back I felt a little flat, but not really depressed. I realised I was looking forward to getting home.

Next day, I paid a final visit to Harajuku with my girlfriend. The street was closed to traffic on Sunday and lots of young people invade with fashions and radios – '50s-meets-punk. We had a light lunch of *sashimi* – raw fish – in a little bar where a group of men were watching horse-racing on TV. There was excitement when one of them realised he had won 70,000 yen – about £200.

In the afternoon, I went to see Toshi and Chica's group Plastics rehearsing. They played very jerky music to strange but simple chord sequences with Chica shouting shrill words of protest in Japanese and English. Their drummer operated a primitive drum machine. I think 'puppet rock' is how I would tag them. There was a piano in one corner so I even got to play with them. It was fun, and I'd love to have done a gig.

We all went back to the hotel in a couple of cars. I played them a tape of Fumble, very different from what we had just been playing! They looked through my photos and we chatted while I finished most of my packing – an impossible task. I ended up giving them half my stage clothes before I could squeeze the cases shut. We arranged to meet again later.

That evening I met Tetsu, who used to play bass with the Faces. He looked drawn and older, with a wispy oriental moustache, a more subdued character. He was friendly, but withdrawn at first. The talk drifted to our early days in music. He had been in a small band on the road in Europe at the same time as Fumble. We both remembered the Reading Festival in 1973 – hot from Bowie's American tour, Fumble had wakened up the afternoon crowd. That night the Faces were topping, Tetsu's first big gig with them. Now he was making an album of Japanese music. He didn't expect it to be a big success, but in his heart this was what he wanted to do.

I met up with Plastics again outside the Crazy Horse, a big club in Ropongi. It was late, and the only places to eat were hamburger joints, a big let-down on my last night in Japan! So Toshi asked me diffidently if I would come back to his parents' house, and perhaps his mother could cook us something. I agreed readily – it is unusual to be invited to a Japanese household and I felt very privileged.

We left our shoes just inside the door. The house was not really small, but had a look of being miniature, very delicate. I felt that the screen walls would fall down if I sneezed. I met his parents and his sister, Noriko. His father, in vest and braces, bowed to me and shortly disappeared. His mother was plump and jolly with a few words of English. She made us all very welcome, producing tea and little cakes, then went off into the kitchen. We all talked, and I told them about recording with David.

A little later Mum appeared with an apron on and showed us into the dining-room. There was just a low table and no chairs, and I wondered how I was going to manage. But they lifted the quilted tablecloth and a red light shone out from underneath - the table covered a square pit in the floor with a heater, and we sat dangling our legs, the quilted cloth sealing in the warmth. Noriko and Mum soon covered the table in dishes, a feast I had not been expecting, and Chica knelt beside me in traditional style, deftly serving me with a pair of chopsticks.

It was a delicious meal and I felt overwhelmed to be treated like this. When I was leaving, Toshi's mother presented me with two traditional printed cloths and a box of home-made cakes for my mother. All I could give in return was my Elvis badge - Mum was a fan!

Monday, 18th December

Next morning, feeling pretty shattered, Toshi, Chica and I went to the National Theatre to see a traditional puppet play. *Bunraku*, as the art is called, uses puppets twelve feet high, each controlled by three men in black hooded robes, whose presence you must ignore. Today's performance was for schools and included a film and demonstration. We were shown how they carve the elaborate heads which can talk, frown and move their eyes – some even change into monsters or split luridly in half at the blow of a sword.

The stage was very wide and as the large figures took possession of it, I soon hardly noticed their black-clad supporters. At one side a musician twanged a three-stringed guitar while another produced an extraordinary range of nasal voices. This strange music induced an atmosphere of hypnotic intensity and the mood was sometimes heightened by the desiccated rattle of a wood-block off-stage. It was an unusual and memorable experience.

Outside it was very cold, this mid-December day being the first breath of winter I had felt on this tour. We took a taxi back and had a quick 'lunch-box' meal, a selection of cold foods in a lacquer tray. Walking back towards the hotel, we dived into a pinball parlour where they introduced me to the game of Space Invaders which was just sweeping Japan. Then we said goodbye.

I finished my packing, a final squeeze, leaving behind a full bottle of Chevas Regal, a tube of toothpaste I didn't dare squeeze, and half a dozen LPs from the sleeves which David had autographed. At 6.30am a young porter helped me down with my case. He asked me if I was a musician, then shook my hand. "I'm very lucky," he said, and I was left wondering if he meant he was lucky meeting me, or that *I* was lucky to be a musician. Hiro, one of Mr. Udo's people, was waiting with a car and drove me to the airport through the evening rush-hour.

There was a thorough security check of all my cases – unusual, because they only check carry-on bags elsewhere. I hauled my cases to the check-in desk and put them on the scales – they were more than 20 kilos overweight, and at 5000 yen per kilo they wanted to charge me £270. I thought about unpacking and dumping my least valuable property in the nearest litter bin – worn boots, second-hand paperbacks. Finally the girl said she would only charge me for 10 kilos so I handed over £130 with some relief – it was the only time I got stung on the whole tour.

I was flying via Alaska, first-class. As I boarded the JAL jumbo, quiet Japanese music reminded me of the puppet play.

We left Japan at 11.30pm, Monday 18th December. I dozed for several hours till an electric dawn revealed a landscape of ice beneath us... Alaska! There was no sense of dimension to the smooth mountains and still, grey lakes, or to the clear white plains and dark cracks of rivers.

"22 degrees Fahrenheit at Anchorage," the pilot announced, "5 below zero, Centigrade."

I perched on the front seat, nose pressed to the cold window, camera at the ready. The musak returned – 'Rudolph The Red-Nosed Reindeer' on a piccolo! Now we had blue-white fog, it was disconcerting, snow on the runway, five below zero and freezing fog! Any other airport would be closed. Then it was cabin lights out, wheels down, the landing lights cast a yellow glare. A snow-bound airport is an awe-inspiring sight!

TOKYO

It was 4.17am, Tuesday, Tokyo time, but 9.17am, Monday, Alaska time. We spent three long hours in the transit lounge while furry parkered 'eskimos' serviced the plane. I bought a woolly ALASKA bobble hat from the souvenir shop which sold jade Eskimo carvings from Taiwan and the USSR, and sent a Merry Christmas postcard to Fumble, though I would arrive before it. At last we took off again, flying due north. The sun dropped away behind us and we entered the endless arctic night to fly over the Pole.

Tuesday, 19 December

Arr. 6.20am Heathrow. Customs v. easy. £30 duty but no search. Meet Mum - snack breakfast. Taxi to flat.

CODA

During the next couple of years, I saw David and Coco quite often when they were in town. One evening I ate strawberries in their suite at The Ritz overlooking the Thames, and heard *Lodger* for the first time. A year later I sat on the floor in a Knightsbridge flat and heard *Scary Monsters*. David was depressed – as he always is after completing a project. He was sure it was terrible and would be a failure. But then he laughed and said this was how he always felt!

We went to various new-wave gigs, met in up-market clubs, queued in a fish and chip shop. Late one Saturday night, David, Coco, Iggy and some of the Australian support group Angel City descended on me after a party and I crawled out of bed and made them all coffee. (I think that was the time David broke my bathroom door.) Another night we went to see Lou Reed and they ended up having a fight in a smart French restaurant.

It was five years before David toured again – 'The Serious Moonlight – Best of Bowie' tour. I had just joined Tom Robinson's band, 'War Baby' was coming out, and I knew if David had asked me to play it would have been, "Thanks – but no thanks!" When the tour hit town, Carlos called me and I went around to the Hilton and told him how many tickets I'd like.

I saw Adrian again on the final old-numbers tour. Coco told me David would like to see me after the gig – they were going to a club on Leicester Square. I went along with a couple of friends and somehow negotiated the security net, alone. Then I thought, *What am I doing? I hate all this – the bouncers in penguin suits, the crush of people trying for a quick word.* And I haven't spoken to David in years – what are we going to talk about? So I returned to my friends outside the club.

This event just confirmed something I had known for years: there is more to life than being 'the guy who played piano for David Bowie'. That is not a sour response, more of a self affirmation! There is more to life, and I'm getting on with it!

That doesn't mean I never look back. It was a very special year, it was a lot of fun, and I am still proud to have been a part of it. And sometimes if the mood takes me, I put on my cassette of *Stage* (re-recorded in the right order), lean back, close my eyes and remember...

THE 1978 WORLD TOUR

(Where no capacity is shown, none is available)

March

USA

Mon 13	Dallas – rehearsals	
Wed 29	San Diego, Sports Arena	15,000 capacity
Thu 30	Phoenix, Coliseum	15,000

April

Sun 2	Fresno, Convention Centre	7,500
Mon 3	Los Angeles, The Forum	18,894
Tue 4	Los Angeles, The Forum	18,894
Wed 5	San Francisco, Oakland Coliseum	14,200
Thu 6	Los Angeles, The Forum	18,894
Sun 9	Houston, The Summit	18,000
Mon 10	Dallas, Convention Centre	10,500

Tue 11	Baton Rouge, LSU Assembly Centre	11,000
Thu 13	Nashville, Municipal Auditorium	9,000
Fri 14	Memphis, Mid-South Coliseum	12,000
Sat 15	Kansas City, unknown venue	5,000
Mon 17	Chicago, Auditorium Theatre	4,000
Tue 18	Chicago, Auditorium Theatre	4,000
Thu 20	Detroit, Cobo Arena	12,000
Fri 21	Detroit, Cobo Arena	12,000
Sat 22	Cleveland, unknown venue	30,000
Mon 24	Milwaukee, Exposition Centre	12,000
Wed 26	Pittsburgh, Civic Arena	
Thu 27	Washington, Landover Capitol Centre	18,000
Fri 28	Philadelphia, The Spectrum	19,500
Sat 29	Philadelphia, The Spectrum	19,500

May
CANADA
Mon 1	Toronto, Maple Leaf Gardens	18,800
Tue 2	Ottawa, Civic Centre	10,000
Wed 3	Montreal, The Forum	18,000

USA
Fri 5	Providence Civic Centre	13,200
Sat 6	Boston, Garden	15,000
Mon 8	New York, Madison Square Garden	20,000
Tue 9	New York, Madison Square Garden	20,000

GERMANY
| Sun 14 | Frankfurt, Festhalle | 1,000 |

Mon 15	Hamburg, Congress Centrum	3,000
Wed 17	Berlin, Deutschlandhalle	10,000
Thu 18	Dusseldorf, unknown venue	
Fri 19	Cologne, unknown venue	
Sat 20	Munich, Olympiahalle	9,000

AUSTRIA

Mon 22	Vienna, Reichstadion	6,200

FRANCE

Wed 24	Paris, Pavilion	8,500
Thu 25	Paris, Pavilion	8,500
Fri 26	Lyon, unknown venue	12,000
Sat 27	Marseilles, unknown venue	

GERMANY - TV

Tue 30	Bremen, Musik–Laden

DENMARK

Wed 31	Copenhagen, Falkoner Theatre	3,000

June

Thu 1	Copenhagen, unknown venue

SWEDEN

Fri 2	Stockholm, unknown venue	
Sun 4	Gothenburg, Scandianvium	8,000

NORWAY

Mon 5	Oslo, Ekberg Hall	5,200

HOLLAND

Wed 7	Rotterdam, Ahoy Sports Palace	7,500
Thu 8	Rotterdam, Ahoy Sports Palace	7,500

Fri 9	Rotterdam, Ahoy Sports Palace	7,500

BELGIUM

Sun 11	Brussels, Forêt National	5,600
Mon 12	Brussels, Forêt National	5,600

BRITAIN

Wed 14	Newcastle, City Hall	2,200
Thu 15	Newcastle, City Hall	2,200
Fri 16	Newcastle, City Hall	2,200
Mon 19	Glasgow, Apollo	3,300
Tue 20	Glasgow, Apollo	3,300
Wed 21	Glasgow, Apollo	3,300
Thu 22	Glasgow, Apollo	3,300
Sat 24	Stafford, Bingley Hall	8,500
Sun 25	Stafford, Bingley Hall	8,500
Mon 26	Stafford, Bingley Hall	8,500
Thu 28	London, Earls Court	15,746
Fri 29	London, Earls Court	15,746
Sat 30	London, Earls Court	15,746

November

SWITZERLAND Montreux, recording

AUSTRALIA

Sun 5	Sydney, rehearsals	
Sat 11	Adelaide, Oval	
Tue 14	Perth, Entertainment Centre	7,500
Wed 15	Perth, Entertainment Centre	7,500
Sat 18	Melbourne, Cricket Ground	

Tue 21   Brisbane, Lang Park

Fri 24   Sydney, Showground

Sat 25   Sydney, Showground

NEW ZEALAND

Wed 29   Christchurch, unknown venue

December

Sat 2   Auckland, Western Springs   41,000

JAPAN

Wed 6   Osaka, Kosei Nenkin Hall

Thu 7   Osaka, Kosei Nenkin Hall

Sat 9   Osaka, Expo Hall

Mon 11   Tokyo, Budokan

Tue 12   Tokyo, NHK Hall